EGG

The very best recipes
inspired by the simple egg

Blanche Vaughan

EGG

EGG

The very best recipes
inspired by the simple egg

Blanche Vaughan

WEIDENFELD & NICOLSON

CONTENTS

INTRODUCTION

'Hen's eggs be the best eggs, and the best be those that be fresh.'

14TH CENTURY COOKBOOK

Where would we be without eggs? Their versatility has made them the foundation of recipes from all over the world. We eat them in many different guises: for breakfast, lunch, tea and supper. This simple ingredient is the star of the kitchen.

We rarely see an egg in its nest, let alone have the pleasure of eating an egg freshly laid. A new egg is one of the most delicious things you can eat and even more enjoyable if you've plucked it from the nest yourself and felt it warm in your hand.

It's often the star of the show, whether baked with chilli and cheese or poached in wine in the classic dish *oeufs en meurette*. But the egg is also a chameleon, taking on many roles: it can be cooked whole or beaten, whisked to make airy cakes and snowy meringues or used in luxurious custards and silky pasta as well as being the crucial binding ingredient in pastries and batters.

Soft-boiled, gently poached, crisp-fried or creamy and scrambled, the breakfast egg has become an institution, and I can't think of a better way to start the day. There are recipes here to bring out the best flavours of the morning egg: anchovy soldiers to dip into runny yolks, eggs scrambled with Spanish black pudding or fried with spices, herbs and chilli. For sweeter days, there are muffins with fruit and fluffy pancakes to cover with crunchy bacon and maple syrup.

At lunchtime, eggs are quick to prepare, the ultimate convenience food: poached with kale and chorizo, turned into fritters with courgette and sumac or used for prepare-ahead dishes such as tortilla or quiche, to be enjoyed warm or cold.

There are cakes and biscuits for teatime; and supper dishes that are both light and substantial - egg pastas, fish dishes with egg sauces and a simple recipe for Japanese chicken and egg.

Puddings put eggs to their most decadent uses, from soufflés and mousses to trifle, crêpes, meringues, steamed puddings and, of course, rich, custard-based ice creams.

A high cholesterol content (according to recent studies) is no longer something to be feared. Instead, eggs are recommended as an excellent source of protein and are crucial as part of a healthy, balanced diet. They are nutritious enough to eat with just a few vegetables and contain plenty of protein for non-meat eaters too. They are also full of vitamins, great for our eyes and skin, hearts and bones.

Once you've seen and tasted eggs from happily reared chickens that are allowed to peck around outside, eating grubs and natural foods, you will find it hard to buy eggs from battery-reared hens. Many well-produced eggs are now available commercially and most supermarkets stock very good quality free-range and organic eggs. Free-range and organically farmed eggs can cost more, but the benefit is a more flavourful, nutritious ingredient and often one that is easier to cook with: eggs that poach easily because the whites are strong, better structured cakes and deep golden yolks for richer custard and puddings.

Like eggs themselves, the majority of the ingredients required for these recipes are easy to find, or may even be in your store cupboard already. A few capers and cornichons, for example, made into a chopped egg sauce can lift a simply cooked piece of fish or chicken. Many of the dishes take very little time to prepare while others, such as the pear and Marsala trifle on page 157 are better when made in advance.

Despite eggs being one of the most familiar ingredients in the kitchen, I am constantly surprised, delighted and inspired by the variety of recipes they can produce, and I hope you will be too.

EGG KNOW-HOW

Buying

Try to choose organic, free-range eggs whenever you can. Don't be misled by labels such as 'farm fresh' or 'barn eggs', which are generally meaningless – a 'farm fresh' egg may well have been produced on a battery farm while hens from 'barn eggs' are still kept inside. Free-range, organic egg production provides chickens with outside space to exercise as well as natural feed that is free from hormones, artificial pesticides and fertilisers. Not only do they taste better because of this, they are also better to cook with; good-quality eggs have viscous whites and flavourful, rich yolks. Quite simply, birds that have been treated humanely and have been able to forage outdoors lead healthier lives and produce finer eggs.

Different breeds of hen produce eggs with different coloured shells, for instance Marans chickens lay brown eggs while Legbars are light blue. Most importantly they all have their own unique flavour, which is mainly down to the quality of nutrients they eat. A deeper coloured yolk is generally a good indication of that the egg has come from a free-range hen.

Many supermarkets now stock different varieties so try experimenting until you find one that you like (my favourites are Clarence Court Burford Browns). Alternatively, buy them from a farm shop or market and see which you prefer. Eggs are available in various sizes, the most popular being medium and large. *Unless otherwise stated I have used medium eggs throughout this book.* In the UK a medium egg is defined as weighing (still in its shell) between 50g and 60g.

Note: Young children, pregnant women and the elderly should avoid recipes using raw egg whites or lightly cooked eggs.

Storing and freshness

Eggs should be kept in a cool, dry place, ideally in the fridge. Stored in cold conditions, pointy end down, they can last for up to three weeks (but always check the use-by date on the packaging). The best way to store eggs in the fridge is in an airtight container; eggshells are porous so they can absorb other smells easily. Don't be tempted to store eggs in the fridge door where they will be constantly jolted as you open and shut the door – this just makes them deteriorate more quickly.

When baking or using egg whites for whisking, the best results are achieved from eggs that have been allowed to come to room temperature. Take them out of the fridge an hour or so before you need to use them. Alternatively, put them in a glass of warm water for a few minutes.

To test if an egg is fresh (without breaking it) put it in a glass of water. If it sinks right to the bottom, it's very fresh, it if stands up slightly, it is still good to use and if it floats, it is past its best so throw it away. Alternatively, break the egg into a glass and have a look at the viscosity of the white and the pertness of the yolk. A slack, watery white and a floppy yolk is an indication of a stale or poor quality egg. If it smells, it definitely needs to go in the bin!

Egg whites freeze very well and can be kept in the freezer for up to three months. A useful tip is to freeze them in small quantities or individually so you don't end up defrosting more than you need; simply tip into an airtight container and make sure you label them with the number of whites and the date. One medium egg white weighs approximately 35g – this is useful to know if you have forgotten to label your frozen egg whites. Thaw frozen egg whites in the fridge overnight. Defrosted egg whites whisk very well, making them ideal for meringues, and can be used in exactly the same way as you would use fresh egg whites. Leftover yolks should be covered and kept in the fridge for up to a week but they don't freeze successfully. Whole eggs, lightly beaten, can also be frozen but I have never seen the point of this; if I need to use up some eggs I just make something.

Separating

Firstly, make sure your hands are thoroughly clean and free from grease. A good firm tap on the edge of a bowl will crack the shell cleanly. Carefully prise open the egg so that you have two even halves. Pass the yolk between each half shell until all of the white has dropped down into the bowl. If you are separating a large number of eggs, for example if you are whisking whites for a meringue, it is safer to separate each egg individually in another container or bowl. This is because any flecks of the yolk will stop the whites from foaming properly. There is nothing more frustrating than separating five eggs perfectly and then breaking the yolk of the final one in the bowl. If any trace of yolk or piece of shell slips in, the best way to remove it is by using half of the broken shell as a scoop. This useful trick does seem to work - the sharp edge of the shell cuts through the viscous white, allowing you to scoop up the piece of shell easily.

Whisking whites

You don't need to use the freshest egg whites for whisking. I've found the most voluminous whisked whites have been produced by slightly older eggs or whites that have been previously frozen (see above). If you have been making yolk-based recipes, always save the whites. They will keep, covered, in the fridge for a few days or in the freezer for up to three months.

Many people are nervous about whisking egg whites but there are some simple tips you should follow for perfectly whisked whites:

- Grease is the enemy of voluminous egg whites as it prevents them from ever building sufficient air bubbles, so remember to keep everything thoroughly clean.
- Avoid plastic or wooden bowls which tend to absorb grease; a metal or glass bowl with a rounded bottom is ideal.
- Bring your eggs to room temperature before whisking.
- If you are using an electric whisk, start on a slow speed, gradually moving up to a higher setting.
- Move the beaters around the bowl as you whisk; they should start to form soft and then stiff peaks. Be careful not to whisk beyond the stiff peak stage as the egg whites will become grainy and lumpy and you'll have to start again.
- Adding sugar, for example when making meringue, helps to stabilise the egg whites, reducing the risk of over-whisking.

BASICS

Boiled eggs

One of the simplest ways to cook an egg is to boil it, in its shell, in water. Soft-boiled eggs, also known as *mollet* eggs, have a creamy, soft white and runny yolk and can be eaten in the shell or peeled and used as a substitute for poached eggs.

There are three things to bear in mind when you are boiling eggs:
· the temperature of the egg when it goes into the water
· the size of the egg
· the speed at which the water boils.
I like to keep eggs in the fridge, because it's safer and they last longer, but they will take a little more time to cook than if they're at room temperature. The most important thing to remember when boiling eggs is to put them into rapidly boiling water, then turn it down and cook them on a low-medium heat, so they don't get bashed around in the pan, which will result in cracked shells.

Bring a pan of water to the boil and carefully put the eggs straight from the fridge into the pan. Reduce the temperature to low-medium so that the water is gently boiling, rather than vigorously bubbling and set your timer. For medium eggs at fridge temperature, use the guide below:
· runny yolk - 5 minutes
· set yolk - 8 minutes
· hard-boiled - 12 minutes
For eggs at room temperature or for smaller or larger eggs, adjust the cooking times by about a minute.

Remove eggs from the pan with a slotted spoon.

Tips for peeling boiled eggs
· The freshest eggs are often the most difficult to peel. If you're intending to peel the eggs, it's best to use those you've had in the fridge for a couple of days. The fresher the egg, the more tightly the shell sticks to the cooked white, causing it to tear when you try to peel it away.
· I find that leaving eggs to cool for too long also makes them harder to peel. Run the eggs under cold water as soon as they are cooked, just long enough so that they can be handled comfortably. Peeling them either submerged in cold water or under a running tap makes the job a lot easier.

Poached eggs

There are many differing opinions about how to achieve the 'perfect' poached egg, which should be an opaque oval of egg white surrounding a soft, runny yolk.

The most important thing to remember is to use the freshest eggs possible. A very fresh, good-quality egg has a thick, gelatinous white, which forms one jellified whole and doesn't disperse in streaks when it is dropped into the water.

Bring a pan of water to a simmer and add a good pinch of salt and a teaspoon of vinegar (optional).

Crack the egg into a glass or cup.

Stir the water a couple of times and slip the egg into the centre of the whirlpool.

Keeping the water at a barely bubbling simmer, cook the egg for 2-3 minutes, or until the yolk is still runny but the white is opaque and just firm.

Use a slotted spoon to scoop out the egg and dab off any excess water with kitchen paper.

Tips on poaching eggs

· Cracking the egg into a glass or cup before poaching gives you a chance to see the quality of the white. If the white is jellified and thick and clings to the yolk, you should have no trouble just sliding it into a pan of simmering, lightly salted water.
· If the eggs are very fresh, you can cook several at a time in undisturbed, simmering water; just make sure there's plenty of room so they don't touch.
· Adding vinegar and/or salt to the poaching water will help the egg white to coagulate. However, unless you start with a good, fresh egg in the first place, you'll be fighting a losing battle.
· If your egg white is a little thinner and not as gelatinous, you can help things along by giving the water a quick swirl with a spoon to create a whirlpool effect. Simply drop the egg into the centre of the whirlpool, although it can be tricky to cook more than one egg at a time using this method.
· If you insist on poaching an egg that is slightly past its peak condition or if you want to poach several eggs at once, an alternative method is to put about 4cm of water in pan or a high-sided frying pan and sit metal ring cutters on the base. Crack an egg into each ring, turn the heat down to a gentle simmer and poach for 3-4 minutes. The white will be contained in the mould and although it may look artificially round, the textural effect is similar.

Fried eggs

There are two ways to fry eggs: slow or fast. Slow-fried eggs produce a set but soft white. Fast-fried eggs produce a frilly, crisp white, crunchy and browned at the edges. Either way the yolk can be runny or hard, as you like it.

I like my slow-fried eggs to be cooked in butter. The heat should be kept at low or medium so that it never reaches a temperature high enough to cause the butter to burn. You need a generous amount of butter, bubbling around the sides of the white, enough that a pool collects when the pan is tilted, allowing you to spoon a little over the top of the egg to encourage cooking.

Fast-fried eggs are all about sizzle and spit and are usually best fried in oil, or a mixture of butter and oil, so the temperature can get really hot. Eggs cooked in this way suit all kinds of savoury dishes, as an embellishment to a bowl of ratatouille, for example, or slid onto a slice of ham in a Breton galette.

Slow

Put a large knob of butter into a non-stick frying pan or skillet over a medium heat and melt until bubbling. Gently crack the egg into the pan and season it well with salt and pepper.

Let it bubble away for a few minutes to allow the white to set. If the butter starts to spit or sizzle, turn down the heat.

When the white has just set, tilt the pan and use a spoon to scoop the hot butter over the still uncooked white around the yolk. Continue spooning over the hot butter until the yolk has reached the desired consistency.

Fast

Heat a couple of tablespoons of oil (olive, sunflower or groundnut) and a large knob of butter in a non-stick frying pan or skillet over a high heat.

When the butter is foaming, crack in the egg (be careful as the oil may spit) and season with salt and pepper.

The white will quickly start to brown and crisp around the edges. After a minute or so of cooking over a high heat the yolk will begin to set.

Transfer to a plate lined with kitchen paper to drain any excess oil.

Scrambled eggs

Scrambled eggs should be cooked over a medium to low heat, stirring continuously so as to create soft curds throughout, rather than having them creamy on top and overcooked underneath.

I find that adding liquid such as cream or milk to the eggs before cooking can make the finished texture a bit watery. Adding a knob of butter just before they finish cooking not only enriches them but also helps prevent the eggs from over-cooking. Once they've stopped cooking, they can be kept warm happily in a low oven or in a dish set over a pan of hot water (a bain-marie).

serves 1

3 eggs, lightly beaten
30g unsalted butter
Sea salt and freshly ground black
   pepper

Lightly beat the eggs and season with a little salt and pepper.

Melt half of the butter in a pan over a medium heat and let it start to foam before pouring in the beaten eggs. Don't worry if the butter browns a little, it will make the eggs taste even better.

Stir the eggs with a spatula or wooden spoon, moving it continuously across the bottom of the pan until they have formed soft curds. Remove from the heat and stir in the remaining butter – this will help stop the eggs from overcooking.

Serve piled onto hot buttered toast.

Omelette

Much has been written about making omelettes, but as Elizabeth David said, 'there is only one infallible recipe for the perfect omelette: your own'. However, if you're reading these pages because you haven't yet settled upon your fail-safe method, here are a few tips that I find very useful.

- Use a pan that things don't stick to. This doesn't necessarily have to be 'non-stick', just something with a good solid base that conducts heat evenly.
- Don't be tempted to put too many eggs into the pan at once. For one person a two-egg omelette cooked in a 20–23cm pan will give you the ideal thickness, about half a centimeter.
- Less is more when it comes to adding to omelettes. Keep to just small amounts of your chosen ingredient.

serves 1

2 eggs
15g butter
Your chosen filling (optional)
Sea salt and freshly ground black
   pepper

Crack the eggs into a bowl and lightly beat with a fork to break the yolks. Dice about half the butter and stir into the beaten eggs, then season with salt and pepper.

Place a 23cm frying pan on a high heat and melt the remaining butter in it, swirling so it covers the whole surface and the sides of the pan.

Pour the eggs into the pan, tilting the pan so the eggs cover the bottom in a thin, even layer. Use a fork to 'agitate' the eggs and circulate the heat from the bottom of the pan.

When the eggs start to set, use the side of the fork to lift up the edge of the omelette, tilting the pan so the uncooked mixture can flow underneath. The surface will become gently ruckled. As soon as the omelette is almost set but still wet on top, fold it in three. (If you are adding a filling, lay a small amount in the middle of the omelette before folding.) Cook for a few more seconds before sliding onto a warm plate.

A few good things to add to omelettes
- Shredded sorrel or chopped fresh herbs
- Sautéed mushrooms
- Fresh crabmeat
- Chopped tomatoes and basil

Frittatas and tortillas
Frittatas and tortillas differ from omelettes mainly in their thickness. They use many more eggs, and other ingredients are suspended in the egg mixture, as opposed to an omelette, which is gently folded over a filling. Omelettes are cooked so that the egg on top is still slightly runny and are served hot, whereas frittatas and tortillas are mostly cooked through and are delicious served cold. They are too thick to fold like an omelette, so are usually sliced into wedges.

An Italian frittata is generally cooked in a pan on top of the stove and then finished under a hot grill or in the oven to give a puffed-up, browned top.

Tortillas are similar to frittatas but a classic Spanish tortilla should always contain potato. They are usually turned out of the pan and inverted to cook on the other side, rather than finished in the oven.

Rich pasta dough

Making your own pasta is an opportunity to create pasta that is much silkier and richer than the commercially produced, dried varieties. Try to use the best quality eggs with bright orange yolks, which will give the pasta a wonderful golden colour. For best results use fine milled flour, also known as '00' flour, although you can use plain flour as an alternative. This is also one recipe where you will need a piece of equipment: a pasta machine.

I tend to make smaller quantities if I'm making fresh pasta, so it's not too much of a palaver when it comes to rolling it out. But for larger numbers, just multiply the recipe as required.

serves 4

300g '00' flour (this is fine milled
    pasta flour, or use plain flour
    as an alternative)
½ tsp fine sea salt
10 egg yolks
fine semolina flour, for dusting
    (or extra plain flour)

Put the flour and salt into a large bowl and make a well in the centre. Add all the yolks and mix with a fork, until the mixture starts to come together to form a crumbly dough. Use your hands to bring the pieces together to form one mass, adding a few teaspoons of cold water if it is too dry. (You can also use an electric mixer with a dough hook for this stage.)

When you have a cohesive dough, knead it gently on a lightly floured surface for about 5 minutes. Wrap in cling film and chill for at least 30 minutes before rolling in a pasta machine.

When you are ready to roll, liberally dust your work surface with flour.

Divide the dough into three equal-sized pieces and squash them into flattish discs.

Put the pasta machine on its widest setting and roll one of the discs of dough through it. Fold the sheet into three (so that you have a rough rectangle), turn it 90 degrees and roll it through the machine again. Repeat this a couple of times before reducing the setting by one notch. Keep rolling until eventually the machine is two up from its thinnest setting.

Fold the sheet to the same width as the machine, then increase the setting to the widest and send it through a couple more times.

Then reduce the setting of the machine and continue to roll the sheet through, decreasing the setting every time, until you reach the thinnest. By this stage the dough should be smooth and silky.

If the sheet becomes too long and difficult to handle, cut it into shorter lengths.

When the pasta has been rolled through the machine on its thinnest setting, lay the sheet on your floured work surface to dry slightly and continue with the rest of the dough.

When all the dough has been rolled into sheets, cut them into 25cm lengths. You can either cut them into ribbons, using the ribbon cutting attachment on the machine, or by hand, into whichever shape you choose.

Put the cut pasta on a flat plate or tray, well dusted with semolina flour, until you are ready to cook it. Fresh pasta can be kept for 24 hours in the fridge.

Alternative flour pasta dough

Another good reason to make your own pasta is that it gives you the chance to experiment with different flours. Spelt and Khorasan (or Kamut) flours are made from ancient grains, which have not been developed and refined like most modern wheat varieties. They produce very different textures and flavours which complement different sauces; pasta made with spelt flour is softer and silkier (great with fonduta, see page 132) while Khorasan has a nuttier, more wholesome flavour that works well with stronger flavours (see the recipe for kamut pasta with bottarga and celery, page 134).

Not only are spelt and Khorasan flours more nutritious than ordinary plain flour, they are also easier to digest and people with gluten or wheat intolerances are often able to eat them as alternatives.

serves 4

200g spelt flour, fine milled or
    Khorasan flour (such as Kamut)
¼ tsp fine sea salt
2 whole eggs
2 egg yolks
Fine semolina flour, for dusting
    (or the flour used for the dough)

Put the flour and salt into a bowl and make a well in the centre. Add the eggs and egg yolks and mix with a fork, until the mixture starts to come together to form a crumbly dough. Use your hands to bring the pieces together to form one mass, adding a few teaspoons of cold water if it is too dry. (You can also use an electric mixer with a dough hook for this stage.)

When you have a cohesive dough, knead it gently on a lightly floured surface for about 5 minutes. Wrap in cling film and chill for at least 30 minutes before rolling in a pasta machine.

When you are ready to roll, liberally dust your work surface with fine semolina flour, spelt or Khorasan flour.

Divide the dough into three equal-sized pieces and squash them into flattish discs.

Put the pasta machine on its widest setting and roll one piece of the dough through it. Fold the sheet into three (so that you have a rough rectangle), turn it through 90 degrees and roll it though the machine again. Repeat this about 10 times and you will see the dough becoming softer and silkier as you go.

Then reduce the setting on the machine and continue to roll the sheet through the rollers, reducing the width of the setting each time.

If the sheet becomes too long and difficult to handle, cut it into shorter lengths, about 25cm long.

When the pasta has been rolled through the machine on its thinnest setting, lay the sheet on your floured work surface to dry slightly and continue with the rest of the dough.

When all the dough has been rolled into sheets, cut them into 25cm lengths. To use, either cut the pasta sheets into ribbons, using the ribbon cutting attachment on your pasta machine, or, by hand, into whichever shape you choose.

Cleared stock

Egg whites are used in a completely different way here – this time to transform cloudy stock into sparkling, clear liquid. A cleared stock is one that has had the solid particles removed or 'cleared', perfect for making consommés or clear broth and when the stock is set in jelly, the appearance is crystal and transparent throughout. A cleared stock with this quality of flavour is essential for making the oeufs en gelée on page 127.

makes about 1.5 litres stock

1 whole chicken, about 1.5kg
4 rashers streaky bacon
2 carrots, peeled and chopped
1 onion, halved, skin on
3 celery sticks, chopped
1 leek, rinsed and chopped
½ celeriac, chopped
Bouquet garni
1 bay leaf
1 tsp black peppercorns

3 egg whites and shells

Put the whole chicken into a pan large enough to fit it comfortably and add all the other ingredients apart from the egg whites and shells. Pour over enough cold water to cover and place it over a high heat. Bring to the boil, use a spoon to remove any scum from the surface. Reduce the heat and simmer for 15 minutes then take the pan off the heat and allow to cool completely.

When the stock has cooled, remove the whole chicken; the poached chicken meat can be eaten cold (served with the poached vegetables on page 122, or used in pies or other chicken dishes).

Strain the stock and taste it (it's good to taste it before and after reducing, so you can get a sense of how much the flavour has increased). Place over a high heat, bring to the boil and reduce by about half until the flavour has really intensified.

Pour the reduced stock into a clean pan and add the egg whites and shells. Bring to the boil, stirring with a whisk. As soon as it comes to the boil, stop stirring and turn off the heat. The whites and shells will solidify and form a crust on the surface; do not stir past this point.

Bring to the boil again and turn off the heat. Repeat this process one more time.

Strain through a muslin or jelly bag, discarding the egg white crust and any sediment.

Store in a clean container in the fridge for up to 3 days or freeze until needed.

Sweet pastry

This recipe uses a different method to other pastries to produce a lighter, crisper texture, suitable for use in sweet tarts. The flour is added right at the end preventing it from getting over-worked. For a wholemeal sweet pastry, see the recipe for Seville orange tartlets on page 112.

makes 1 × 23cm tart shell

80g unsalted butter
50g caster sugar
Pinch fine sea salt
1 egg yolk
160g plain flour, plus extra
    for dusting

Mix the butter and sugar with a pinch of salt in an electric mixer or in a large bowl with a hand-held blender, until smooth and creamy.

Add the yolk and continue to mix so it is well combined.

Add the flour and mix briefly, then scoop the mixture into a clean bowl, add a tablespoon of cold water and using your hands, bring the pastry together. Add another tablespoon of water if necessary to form a cohesive but firm dough.

Wrap in cling film and allow to rest for at least an hour or overnight in the fridge.

On a lightly floured surface, roll out the pastry until it is large enough to fit your tart tin. Line your tin, keeping any pastry offcuts in case you need to plug any holes after blind baking.

Note: Pastry freezes well, either wrapped in cling film before rolling, or once you have lined your tart tin (it can be baked from frozen). If you have frozen your pastry in a ball, simply defrost just enough to allow you to grate it straight into your tart tin. It can then be pressed into the base and sides of the tin by hand.

Custard

Custard, or crème anglaise, is often made using only the egg yolks, but here I've used whole eggs as well as yolks, which produces a lighter custard - perfect for pouring.

makes 500ml

100ml full-fat milk
200ml single cream
1 vanilla pod
3 whole eggs
2 egg yolks
60g caster sugar

Pour the milk and cream into a pan. Cut the vanilla pod in half lengthways and scrape the seeds into the pan (keep the pod to flavour a jar of caster sugar to make vanilla sugar).

Bring the milk and cream just to boiling point and then turn off the heat.

In a large bowl, whisk the eggs, egg yolks and sugar until light and creamy. Slowly pour the hot cream into the bowl, whisking all the time, then return the whole lot to the pan. Cook over a low heat to thicken, stirring all the time. It is ready when it coats the back of the spoon.

Troubleshooting

Eggs - the magic ingredients that thicken custard - can also cause problems; if the heat is too high they will curdle. If this starts to happen, immediately remove the pan from the heat and whizz the custard with a handheld stick blender until smooth. If you don't have a handheld stick blender, plunge the pan into a bowl of iced water and whisk energetically by hand. (It is worth having a bowl of iced water at the ready, in case this happens.)

Crème patissière

Crème patissière is custard that has been thickened with flour. This not only changes the texture, but it stabilises it too, which means that it can be boiled without fear of splitting.

As well as providing one of the layers in a trifle, it can be used as filling for profiteroles, spread over a pastry shell and topped with fruit, or sandwiched in a brioche bun. Here I've flavoured it with a vanilla pod, but vanilla extract can also be used, as well as other flavours such as lemon zest, cinnamon or cocoa powder.

150ml single cream
150ml full-fat milk
1 vanilla pod
4 egg yolks
40g caster sugar
1 tbsp plain flour

Put the cream and milk into a saucepan. Split the vanilla pod lengthways and scrape the seeds into the pan (keep the pod and add to a jar of caster sugar to make vanilla sugar).

Bring the cream and milk just to boiling point and then immediately turn off the heat and leave to infuse.

Meanwhile, whisk the yolks, sugar and flour in a large bowl until they are creamy and thick. Slowly pour the hot cream into the bowl, whisking all the time.

Return the mixture to the pan and continue to whisk over a high heat while it comes to the boil. Keep cooking for another minute or so as it bubbles and thickens.

Remove from the heat and transfer to a clean bowl set over ice, to cool. If any lumps have formed during the cooking, just pass the custard through a sieve to remove them.

BREAKFAST

Soft-boiled egg with anchovy toast

serves 1

1-2 eggs, depending on how hungry you are
1 whole salted anchovy, cleaned and filleted
Squeeze of lemon juice
10g unsalted butter
Freshly ground black pepper
Slice of good-quality white bread or sourdough, toasted

This is my favourite way to eat a simple boiled egg: crisp toast soldiers dipped into rich, runny egg yolk. There is something magical about the combination of salty anchovy, buttery toast and warm yolk.

I like to use salted anchovies, rather than those preserved in oil, as they blend more easily into the butter. They come packed in salt and need to be cleaned and filleted, which is easier than it sounds: just rinse them gently in water and remove the backbone with your fingers. Anchovies in oil will also work if you haven't got salted ones; just make sure you drain them well. It's worth making a larger batch of anchovy butter as it keeps for up to a week in the fridge and means that breakfast will be quicker to prepare next time.

_____

Boil the egg(s) to your preferred consistency – I recommend soft-boiled.

While the eggs are cooking, toast your bread and prepare the anchovy butter. Chop the anchovy finely and pound it with the lemon juice in a pestle and mortar, which will cause it to dissolve slightly. Add the butter and pepper, pounding until smooth and spreadable. (If you are using an anchovy in oil, you may need to add some salt at this stage.)

If you don't have a pestle and mortar, you can do this on a chopping board. Chop the anchovy finely and then use the flat side of the knife blade to squash and spread it repeatedly. Transfer to a bowl and use a fork to blend with the lemon juice and then the butter.

Spread the butter on the toast and cut into soldiers.

As soon as the eggs are cooked, crack open the top and get dipping.

Egg in a nest with paprika and za'atar

An egg on toast is one thing, but an egg in toast is another thing entirely. The white seeps into the bread while the yolk is suspended in a nest.

This is a very good recipe for using eggs that are past poaching freshness, as the looser white will absorb into the bread better. Paprika and za'atar taste excellent with eggs but you could easily use other spices or herbs.

serves 2

1 tbsp olive oil
2 large slices of bread (I like to use a good sourdough)
2 eggs
2 large pinches paprika
2 large pinches za'atar
Sea salt and freshly ground black pepper

Cut a circle, about the size of a yolk, out of the middle of each slice of bread (I use my smallest pastry cutter for this).

In a frying pan large enough to fit both slices of bread, heat the oil and fry the bread to brown on one side. Turn it over and crack an egg over each slice, aiming to get the yolk into the hole and the white over the rest of the bread. Sprinkle paprika, za'atar, salt and pepper over each and cover with any lid - you can improvise with a plate if necessary.

Cook for 3-4 minutes (have a peek to see if the white has turned opaque and the yolk is cooked to your liking).

I find a couple of fried or roasted tomatoes go extremely well with this.

Crisp (frizzled) eggs with sage and chilli

serves 2

A mixture of olive oil and
  sunflower oil, to come to a depth
  of 1cm in the pan
About 12 sage leaves
2 eggs
2 pinches dried hot chilli flakes
Toast, to serve
Greek yoghurt, to serve (optional)
Sea salt and freshly ground black
  pepper

This is a very satisfying breakfast when you need to blow the cobwebs away. Once you've got the knack of frizzling, you can try using other flavours with the eggs – ground allspice and parsley, or tarragon and vinegar are other delicious additions.

Heat the oil in a deep frying pan until almost smoking hot. Fry the sage leaves for a few seconds on each side to crisp. Remove and drain on kitchen paper.

Crack each egg into a glass and slip into the hot oil – this will prevent the hot oil splashing as you drop the eggs in. Fry for a few seconds so the edge of the white starts to brown and crisp. When the white becomes opaque and the yolks are still runny, transfer to a plate lined with kitchen paper to drain away any excess oil.

Serve on toast with the sage leaves and chilli flakes sprinkled on top. Season well with salt and pepper. A dollop of thick Greek yoghurt goes very well with this.

Any excess oil can be reused – when completely cool, just strain it into a bottle and seal and store until needed.

Poached eggs on tomato toast with bacon

serves 2

4 rashers of streaky bacon
2 very fresh eggs
2 slices of good bread – I like to use
   rye or sourdough
2 ripe tomatoes, halved
Sea salt and freshly ground black
   pepper

My ultimate egg and bacon breakfast. When tomatoes are in season and sweet and ripe, I make this with fresh ones. At other times of the year, to get that intense flavour, I use halved cherry tomatoes which have been dressed with salt, pepper and olive oil and roasted in an oven at 180°C/350°F/gas mark 4 for an hour.

––––––––––––––––––––––––

Place a frying pan over a high heat and fry the bacon until crisp – streaky bacon won't need any extra fat for frying.

Meanwhile poach the eggs in a pan of simmering water for 3 minutes. Adding a splash of vinegar to the poaching water works well here as the flavour goes nicely with the tomatoes. Remove from the pan and drain on kitchen paper.

Toast the bread. Squash and rub the tomatoes, cut side down, all over the toast so that the flesh squeezes into it. Season well with salt and pepper.

Lay the bacon on top of the tomato toast and pour over any fat from the pan.

Put a poached egg on top of each piece of toast, sprinkle over a little more salt and pepper and serve.

Scotch woodcock

serves 2

6 eggs
Good pinch cayenne pepper
20g unsalted butter
1 tsp small salted capers
1 tbsp freshly chopped flat-leaf
    parsley
4 anchovies in oil, sliced in half
    lengthways
Sea salt and freshly ground black
    pepper
Buttered toast, to serve

This doesn't have a trace of woodcock in it, but I love the name for being so entirely misleading. It's essentially scrambled eggs with anchovies and capers. Scotch Woodcock dates back to Victorian times, when it would be served as a 'savoury', a dish eaten after the main course and before the pudding. I think it makes a great breakfast dish, as well as a good teatime snack. The salty anchovies and capers are the perfect combination with rich, buttery egg.

_____

Lightly beat the eggs and season with a little salt (remember the capers and anchovies will taste salty too), pepper and cayenne.

Melt half the butter in a pan over a medium-high heat and briefly fry the capers before pouring in the eggs. Don't worry if the butter browns a little, it will make the eggs taste even better.

Stir, scraping the bottom of the pan continuously until the eggs have formed soft curds. Stir in the parsley and the remaining butter (this will help stop the eggs from over-cooking).

Remove from the heat and spoon onto the buttered toast. Lay the anchovies over the eggs and serve immediately.

Scrambled eggs with black pudding

serves 4

1 tbsp olive oil
8 slices of black pudding or
    morcilla, cut into dice
10g unsalted butter
8 eggs, lightly beaten
1 tbsp freshly chopped flat-leaf
    parsley
Sea salt and freshly ground black
    pepper

If you can find it, the Spanish blood pudding called 'morcilla', made with rice and spices works wonderfully in this dish, giving the eggs an unusual texture and flavour.

_____

Heat the oil in a frying pan and fry the black pudding slices for a few minutes until they are browned and crisp.

Add half the butter to the pan and then pour in the eggs. Season with salt and pepper and cook, stirring continuously to scrape up the egg as it solidifies on the bottom of the pan.

When the eggs have formed soft curds but are still looking creamy, remove from the heat and stir in the remaining butter and the parsley. They will continue to cook in the residual heat from the pan.

Spoon onto warm plates and serve immediately.

Green eggs

serves 2

1 tbsp olive oil
1 large shallot, finely chopped
1 clove garlic, finely chopped
200g spinach, washed
2 tbsp freshly chopped marjoram
    and flat-leaf parsley
2 eggs
10g butter
2 tbsp Greek yoghurt
Pinch chilli flakes
Sea salt and freshly ground black
    pepper

This is the kind of dish I always want to order when I go to a café for breakfast, but it's never on the menu. And unlike many breakfast egg dishes, this one is good to eat without toast.

If you don't feel like poaching your eggs, try cooking them soft-boiled or *mollet* instead (see page 14).

Heat the oil in a pan with a lid over a medium heat and add the shallots and a pinch of salt. Sauté for a few minutes to soften, then add the garlic and fry for another minute or so.

Throw in the wet spinach and chopped herbs and season well with salt and pepper. Cover with a lid and cook for a few minutes until the spinach wilts completely. Keep warm.

Meanwhile cook your eggs: either poach or soft-boil them.

Cook the butter in a small pan until it starts to brown and smell nutty, remove from the heat and set aside.

When the eggs are cooked either drain them on kitchen paper or gently peel away the shells.

Drain the spinach in a sieve to remove any excess water and then divide between two warmed plates. Add a dollop of yoghurt, place an egg on top of each plate and sprinkle with chilli flakes. Finally pour the brown butter over the top and serve immediately.

Brioche

makes 1 × 900g loaf or 12 small buns

2 tbsp milk
½ sachet (3.5g) fast-action dried
    yeast
250g strong white flour
1 tsp fine sea salt
40g caster sugar
100g unsalted butter, softened
2 whole eggs and 1 egg yolk, lightly
    beaten
Melted butter and flour for the tins

For the glaze
1 egg, beaten
1 tbsp milk

I don't usually go in for making breads that a good bakery will do better. However, I do make an exception for egg-enriched brioche because it's surprisingly easy to make. It can rise overnight while you're asleep, so all you need to do the following morning is put the loaf in the oven and within half an hour you will have warm, buttery brioche for breakfast. Any leftovers can be eaten for tea, toasted and spread with jam, turned into eggy bread or made into bread and butter pudding.

––––––––––––––––––––––––

Put the milk in a small pan and heat gently until it is just tepid, or blood temperature. Dissolve the yeast in the milk, then stir in 1 tablespoon of the flour. Set aside for 15 minutes to allow the yeast to become active and bubbly.

Put the remaining flour, salt and sugar into a large bowl and, using your hands, rub the butter into the flour until it is roughly combined. Make a well in the centre and pour the yeast and milk mixture into the well, along with the beaten eggs. Using your hands, gradually bring the mixture into the centre to incorporate all the wet ingredients. Once it has come together to form a dough, place on a lightly floured board and knead for 5 minutes until you have a smooth, elastic dough.

Prepare your loaf tin or muffin tray by brushing the inside with melted butter and dusting with flour.

Put the dough into the prepared container and leave it to rise at cool room temperature overnight. It will double in size.

The next morning, preheat the oven to 180°C/350°F/gas mark 4.

Combine the beaten egg and milk and use to glaze the brioche. Bake in the preheated oven for about 15 minutes for individual buns or 30-35 minutes for a loaf. To test if the loaf is cooked sufficiently, give it a tap; it should sound hollow. Remove the loaf from the tin and allow to cool slightly before slicing.

Gypsy toast

serves 4-6

200ml milk
1½ tbsp honey
1 clove
Pinch ground cinnamon
1 baguette - even better if it's
    slightly stale (for about 12 slices)
2 eggs, whisked
Knob of butter, for frying
Sugar, to sprinkle

Eggy bread, French toast, *pain perdu*, poor knights of Windsor - you can call it what you like, but at home, my mother always called it Gypsy toast and served it for breakfast. I've tried making it with different styles of bread, but I find baguette is the most successful. The dough has a soft texture and the slices are the perfect size. But if you don't use baguette, it's a good way to use up any leftover or slightly stale white bread.

_____

Put the milk in a pan with the honey, clove and cinnamon and bring to a simmer.

Cut the bread into slices on the diagonal.

Lay the slices in a flat dish so they form one layer and pour the milk over, turning them a couple of times so they can soak on both sides.

As soon as the bread slices have absorbed the milk and the crusts feel soft (this can take between 30 seconds and 2 minutes depending on how stale they are), pour the whisked egg over the bread and turn once to coat on both sides.

Melt the butter in a frying pan over a medium heat and fry the soaked slices until brown, before flipping to cook the other side.

Remove from the pan and sprinkle with sugar to serve.

Drop scones

makes 8-10

120g plain flour (spelt or Kamut
    flour also work well)
1 tsp baking powder
1 tbsp sugar or honey
1 whole egg, beaten
1 egg, separated
2 tbsp natural yoghurt (this makes
    a softer pancake, but can be
    substituted with more milk
    or water)
220ml milk
20g butter, plus extra for frying
mixed berries, to serve (optional)
1 tsp icing sugar, to dust

These are just as good for breakfast, topped with bacon and maple syrup, as they are for tea, slathered in butter and jam.

I like to make the batter the night before so that when I get up in the morning they are ready to cook. If you are making it on the day you should leave it to chill for at least half an hour before cooking - doing this will produce a lighter pancake. If you do make the batter the night before, just don't add the melted butter or whisked egg white until you are about to cook them.

————————————————————

Sift the flour and baking powder into a bowl and add the sugar or honey. Make a well in the centre and pour in the beaten egg, egg yolk (reserving the egg white for later), yoghurt (if using) and milk. Stir to gradually incorporate all the flour until you have a smooth batter, then cover and chill in the fridge for at least 30 minutes, or overnight (see above).

Choose a good non-stick or well-seasoned frying pan and place over a high heat. Melt the 20g of butter in the pan, then pour it into the batter and mix well.

Put the egg white into a large bowl and whisk until it starts to foam, then add the caster sugar and continue to whisk until it forms soft peaks. Gently fold the egg white into the batter.

Return the frying pan to the heat (you shouldn't need to add any more butter) and when it is very hot, pour about half a ladle of batter into the pan. I can usually fit 3-4 dollops of batter in the pan at a time. Cook until small bubbles start to appear on the surface, then flip over to cook on the other side.

When they are ready, pile them on top of each other on a plate and keep warm while you cook the next batch, rubbing a little more butter onto the pan between each batch. Serve with fresh berries, if using, and a dusting of icing sugar.

Also try
· Add mashed banana into the batter before cooking.
· Sprinkle blueberries into the pancakes before you flip
  them over.

Banana, spelt and honey muffins

makes 12

180g spelt flour (plain flour also
    works well)
25g rolled oats
½ tsp fine sea salt
½ tsp bicarbonate of soda
1 tsp baking powder
½ tsp ground cinnamon
50g walnuts, finely chopped
4 tbsp honey
100ml natural yoghurt
60g unsalted butter, melted
3 very ripe bananas (about 460g),
    peeled and roughly squashed
3 eggs, beaten
Zest of ½ orange
1 tsp vanilla extract

If you ever have bananas which are getting overripe in the fruit bowl, turning them into muffins is a satisfying way to put them to good use. The banana and honey give the muffins a natural sweetness (there is no added sugar) and the spelt flour and rolled oats give them a nutty, wholesome flavour. A healthy start to the day.

Preheat the oven to 190°C/375°F/gas mark 5 and lightly butter a 12-hole muffin tray or line with individual paper cases.

Place all the dry ingredients together in a large bowl.

Mix all the remaining ingredients together well in a separate bowl and then add to the dry ingredients and stir to combine.

Spoon into the muffin tray and bake in the preheated oven for 25-30 minutes, or until slightly risen and browned.

Also try
Replace the chopped walnuts with the same amount of pumpkin seeds.

LUNCH

Mozzarella in carozza

makes 6-8 fingers

4 slices of white bread
4 slices of buffalo mozzarella
    (about 1 × 125g ball)
2 eggs
2 tbsp olive oil
Sea salt and freshly ground black
    pepper

Optional extras
2 pinches dried marjoram
Pinch chilli flakes
4 anchovy fillets

You don't need to use fancy bread for this recipe – a basic white bloomer or a soft white bread works best because it can be squeezed to enclose the filling. These mozzarella sandwiches are dipped in egg and then shallow-fried, making them deliciously soft and gooey. They are perfect snacks for children – as well as being a delicious antipasti to serve to adults with drinks.

_____

Cut the crusts off the bread and lay the mozzarella over two of the slices. Season well with salt and pepper.

Sprinkle over dried marjoram, chilli flakes or lay on anchovy fillets, if using.

Top with the remaining slices of bread and squeeze the pieces of bread together to seal, especially around the edges. Cut each sandwich into three or four fingers.

Beat the eggs in a shallow dish and season with salt and pepper. Lay the sandwich fingers in the egg, turning to coat and soak for just a few minutes.

Heat the oil in a frying pan over medium-high heat and fry the sandwiches for a couple of minutes on each side, until they become crisp and brown and the mozzarella starts to ooze out. Sprinkle with salt to serve.

Courgette fritters with dill

serves 4

3 large courgettes (about 450g)
2 tbsp freshly chopped dill
1 tbsp freshly chopped mint
2 tsp sumac
Zest of ½ lemon
2 eggs
Pinch chilli flakes
4 tbsp rice flour (or plain flour)
Sea salt and freshly ground black
    pepper
Vegetable oil for frying (about
    300ml)
Mango chutney, to serve

These crisp fritters are a delicious, quick and healthy light lunch. They can be eaten in your hands, with a dip, or served as a side dish with some simply cooked chicken or fish.

Rice flour gives the batter a lovely texture and it's gluten free, but you can also use plain flour instead. Sumac is a red berry which is usually sold ground; it has a bright, lemony flavour, but if you can't get hold of it, just use some more lemon zest and a tablespoon of the juice.

Coarsely grate the courgettes into a large sieve set over a mixing bowl. Sprinkle with a teaspoon of salt and leave for about 5 minutes, then squeeze out as much of the moisture as you can. Pat dry with kitchen paper and place in a dry bowl.

Add all the other ingredients except the oil and mango chutney and mix well to form a loose batter.

Heat the oil in a deep frying pan until almost smoking - about 180°C/350°F is the best temperature for frying as the food frying in it will crisp nicely without absorbing too much oil. If you don't have a thermometer, a good way to test the oil temperature is to drop a scrap of bread into it. If it sizzles and turns brown in a few seconds then the oil is hot enough.

Drop a spoonful of batter into the pan, pressing down with the back of the spoon to make a little pancake. Repeat with as many more spoonfuls as will fit comfortably in the pan, but take care not to overfill.

Turn each fritter over after a few minutes of cooking. When both sides are golden brown and crisp, transfer to a plate lined with kitchen paper. Continue cooking the fritters in batches until the batter is used up.

You can eat these piping hot or cooled a little - they taste as good either way. Serve with mango chutney.

Also try
Instead of mango chutney, try serving these fritters with a herby yoghurt, for a cooling alternative. Mix a few tablespoons of yoghurt with chopped coriander, mint and parsley, and some salt and pepper.

Beetroot salad with herbs and soft-boiled eggs

serves 2

4 beetroot, washed
Small bunch of thyme sprigs
4 tbsp olive oil
2 soft-boiled (*mollet*) eggs
3 spring onions, chopped
1 tbsp salted capers, rinsed, drained
    and chopped
Small bunch of flat-leaf parsley
    chopped
Small bunch of fresh dill, chopped
2 tbsp sour cream or crème fraîche
1 tbsp wine vinegar
Sea salt and freshly ground black
    pepper

Roasted beetroot has a wonderfully intense, sweet flavour but the long cooking time means it's not ideal when you want a quick salad. I usually roast a whole tray at once, when I have time, and then use the beetroot for different things throughout the week – including this salad, which makes a good lunch dish.

Otherwise, if you don't have time to roast beetroot from raw, pre-cooked beetroot are easy to find, just omit the vinegar in the recipe because they've usually been coated in it already.

————————————————

Preheat the oven to 200°C/400°F/gas mark 6.

Put the unpeeled, raw beetroot into a roasting tray with the thyme sprigs, 2 tablespoons of olive oil, a few pinches of salt and a few tablespoons of water. Cover with foil and roast for 1½–2 hours, or until a knife inserted through the middle meets no resistance.

Remove and allow to cool slightly before slipping off their skins.

Meanwhile cook your soft-boiled eggs.

Cut the beetroot into wedges and put them in a bowl with the spring onions, capers and herbs.

Mix the sour cream with the vinegar and remaining oil, season well and then stir into the beetroot.

Arrange the beetroot salad on a serving dish. Carefully peel the eggs, halve them lengthways and arrange on top.

Tortilla

serves 4-6

6 tbsp olive oil
4-6 large white onions (about
    800g), thinly sliced
900g large, waxy potatoes, such
    as Charlotte or Roosevelt
1 litre sunflower oil
6-7 eggs
Sea salt and freshly ground black
    pepper

A classic Spanish tortilla should be thick enough to slice like a cake. Unlike an omelette, the filling should be 3-4 cm deep in the pan, so choose a small pan to achieve this. This is the simplest version, made with just potatoes and onion. The onions should be sweet and the potatoes soft and most importantly, there should be a tiny bit of runny filling right in the middle.

When I worked at Moro, we used to make tortilla every day for the bar. One of the first things I learned there was how to cook the onions properly: long and slow, so they became unctuous and sweet. It's a great dish to make in advance and tastes just as good eaten cold, served with a beer or taken on a picnic.

_____

I use a 23cm wide frying pan that is at least 5cm deep.

Heat the olive oil in the pan until almost smoking hot before adding the onions so they sizzle as soon as they hit the oil. Season them with a good pinch of salt and stir well. Keep them on a high heat, stirring every now and then until they start to soften, about 5 minutes. If they start to brown, turn down the heat, reduce the temperature.

Continue cooking on a medium-high heat, stirring occasionally, for about 30 minutes. As they cook, they will slowly start to caramelise and turn from yellow to dark gold and become sweet and sticky. The volume will also reduce drastically.

Meanwhile, peel the potatoes, cut them in half lengthways and then slice into evenly sized thin discs (or use a mandoline).

Heat the sunflower oil in a large heavy-bottomed pan to about 150°C or until a scrap of bread dropped into it sizzles and browns immediately.

Fry the potatoes in batches, taking care not to overcrowd the pan, until they are just starting to colour, but before they get brown. They should be soft when cut with a knife. Drain on kitchen paper and season well with salt.

When the onions have reached optimum sweetness (be warned, this can take about 30 minutes) and are gooey and caramelised, scrape them from the pan into a sieve set over a bowl. Allow the oil to drain through (you will use this later).

Mix the potatoes and onions in a bowl. Whisk the eggs, add to the potatoes and onions and using your hands, mix together well. The mixture should feel wet and loose. If not, add another egg. Season to taste - if you're going to eat it cold, remember to season it generously.

Return the onion oil to your tortilla pan and place over a high heat until it is almost smoking. Pour the tortilla mixture into the pan, shaking gently as you go. Reduce the heat to medium and using a spatula or palette knife, tuck the edges in and cook for about 5 minutes to allow the base to set.

To cook the other side, place a plate over the top, invert the pan and then slide the tortilla back into the pan, tucking in the edges again. Cook on this side for another 5 minutes. Then repeat the turning process again, cooking the tortilla for another 5 minutes or so on each side and shaping it after every turn. You will end up with a fat disc, browned on each side with rounded edges. Press it gently, it should feel soft but not squidgy.

Turn onto a plate and cool slightly before cutting into wedges.

Breton galettes with ham, cheese and fried egg

makes 6-8

120g buckwheat flour
60g plain flour
Pinch fine sea salt
220ml milk
220ml water
2 eggs, beaten
1 tbsp butter, plus a little extra
    for frying
6-8 eggs
Dijon mustard
6-8 thin slices of cooked ham
6-8 thin slices of Gruyère
Sea salt and freshly ground black
    pepper

Buckwheat, confusingly, is not related to wheat but comes from the same family as rhubarb, sorrel and knotweed. The flour is made from ground seeds rather that grain, and has an inimitable nutty flavour. It doesn't contain any gluten though, so adding a little plain flour will help the batter hold together.

Savoury rolled pancakes are usually served with a sauce poured over the top, which can make them a bit fussy to make. Here no sauce is needed as you have the runny yolk from the fried egg that is rolled up inside the pancake.

_____

Sift the flours into a bowl and add the salt. Put the milk, water and eggs into a jug and whisk.

Make a well in the centre of the flour and pour the milk mixture in, a bit at a time, stirring with a wooden spoon to gradually bring the flour from the sides until you have a smooth batter. Pour the batter back into the jug and leave to rest for at least 30 minutes.

When you are ready to cook the pancakes, melt the tablespoon of butter in the frying pan you are going to use to cook the pancakes, then pour it into the batter. Give the batter a good stir; it should have the consistency of single cream. If not, add a little more water. The pan will now have a good film of butter in it for you to cook your first pancake.

Make sure the pan is really hot and pour a small amount of batter from the jug into the pan, tilting it all around as you go so that the batter spreads in a very thin layer over the bottom. You can pour back any extra batter into the jug.

Cook for a minute or so and then use a spatula to lift up the sides of the pancake and carefully turn over; cook for another minute on the other side until golden brown.

Use a piece of kitchen paper to rub a tiny bit more butter into the pan before cooking each pancake.

When the pancakes are all cooked, put a little more butter into the pan and fry the eggs, so the white is cooked but the yolks are still runny.

On each pancake, spread some Dijon mustard, lay a piece of ham and cheese on top and put an egg on top of that, then season it with salt and pepper. Roll them up and eat immediately. I like to cut mine just where the yolk is, so it spills through the pancake, like a rich sauce.

Also try
These are delicious served with smoked herring roe or other fish eggs and crème fraîche.

Note: Pancakes can be made in advance and reheated easily. Just stack the cooked galettes on top of each other and cover with baking parchment or cling film and store in the fridge until needed. To reheat, put them in a low oven or heat individually in a frying pan with some butter.

Shirred eggs with tomato and peppers

serves 2

2 tbsp olive oil
1 medium onion, diced
2 cloves garlic, finely chopped
300ml tomato passata
1 tsp tomato purée
Few sprigs of thyme
1 bay leaf
2 red peppers (or one red, one yellow)
½ tsp smoked sweet paprika
1 tbsp freshly chopped flat-leaf parsley
1 tsp freshly chopped marjoram or oregano
2 eggs
Sea salt and freshly ground black pepper
Toast, to serve
Fried bacon or chorizo, to serve (optional)

Shirred eggs are baked in the oven in a flat dish. Their name comes from the type of dish which was originally used to cook them in this way. The eggs are cooked surrounded by a tomato and pepper sauce, piquant with paprika, and the whole dish can be brought bubbling to the table. The sauce can be made in advance so your lunch will only take as long as it takes to cook the egg.

Shallow individual dishes are good for this, but any ovenproof baking dish or small frying pan will work.

Heat the oil in a heavy-bottomed pan over a low-medium heat and add the onion with a good pinch of salt. Cook gently for 5 minutes or until the onions are softened but not coloured.

Add the garlic and cook for another couple of minutes before adding in the tomato passata and purée. Season with another good pinch of salt and some black pepper and throw in the thyme and bay leaf. Allow the sauce to cook for at least 10 minutes so it reduces and thickens.

Meanwhile, place the peppers on a sheet of foil, and put them under a hot grill, turning occasionally so they blacken all over. Remove and wrap them in the foil sheet. After a minute or so, unwrap them and allow to cool before peeling off their charred skins. Cut out the stalks, scrape out the seeds and cut the flesh into thin strips; add these to the sauce.

Preheat the oven to 200°C/400°F/gas mark 6.

Add the paprika and chopped herbs to the sauce and cook for another minute. Taste and adjust the seasoning.

Spoon into your ovenproof dish or dishes and make a couple of indentations in the sauce with the back of a spoon. Crack the eggs into these pockets, sprinkle a little salt and pepper over them and bake in the oven for 8–10 minutes.

Serve with toast and fried bacon or chorizo, if you like.

Airy buckwheat pancakes

makes about 12 small pancakes

80g buckwheat flour
40g plain flour
2 tsp baking powder
2 tsp sea salt
2 whole eggs, beaten
1 tbsp natural yoghurt
150ml beer (fizzy water can also be used)
2 egg whites
Butter, for frying

Unlike a lacy crepe, these pancakes are puffed and airy because of the air from the whisked egg white. The buckwheat and beer give them a lovely savoury flavour that goes very well with smoked fish.

One of my favourite ways to eat these is with smoked eel or other smoked fish, a beetroot salad, horseradish mixed with crème fraîche and crisp bacon.

Sift the flours, baking powder and salt into a bowl and make a well in the centre. Add the beaten egg, yoghurt and beer and using a whisk, stir to gradually incorporate all the flour. When you have a smooth batter, cover and leave to rest for at least 30 minutes.

When you are ready to cook them, whisk the egg white to soft peaks and gently fold into the batter.

Choose a good non-stick or well-seasoned frying pan and put it over a high heat. Melt or brush the base with a little butter and ladle a small amount (about 2 tablespoons) of batter into the pan - the mixture should spread into a small circle then start to puff up. Cook for a few seconds then flip over to cook on the other side.

Pile them up on a warm plate while you cook the rest of the pancakes. Serve warm with smoked fish, salad and horse-radish crème fraîche.

Kale and chorizo on toast with poached egg

serves 4

400g kale, tough stalks removed, roughly chopped
2 tbsp olive oil
200g cooking chorizo, sliced
1 clove garlic, sliced
1 red chilli, seeded and sliced
2 tsp cumin seeds, dry roasted and ground
4 poached eggs
4 slices of toast
Sea salt and freshly ground black pepper

I love to eat this easy, sustaining lunch dish in winter when kale is in abundance. But if you don't fancy using kale, chard or large leaf spinach are good substitutes. Here the eggs are poached, but you could just as easily use a soft-boiled or *mollet* egg instead.

_____

Bring a large pan of salted water to the boil and cook the kale for 4 minutes or until tender. Drain and set aside.

Heat the oil in a frying pan over a medium heat and fry the chorizo slices on both sides until brown. Add the garlic, chilli and cumin and fry a little to soften the garlic, without allowing it to brown.

Add the cooked kale and season to taste. Toss the pan a little to coat everything with the chorizo-flavoured oil.

When you have cooked your eggs, pour a little oil over each slice of toast and cover with the kale and chorizo mixture. Place a poached egg on top of each and serve.

Scrambled eggs with tomatoes and soy sauce

Soy sauce added at the end gives the eggs a deep, savoury flavour, which goes very well with tomatoes. Egg scrambled with tomatoes is a popular dish in China, although there the eggs are stir-fried in a wok, which you could use instead of a frying pan.

_____

serves 2

1 tbsp light flavoured oil, such as rapeseed or sunflower
Large handful of cherry tomatoes, halved
4 eggs, lightly beaten
2-3 tbsp dark soy sauce
Sea salt and freshly ground black pepper

Heat the oil in a frying pan over a medium heat and add the tomatoes and salt and pepper. Fry for a minute or so until they start to soften.

Pour in the eggs and cook, stirring and scraping all the cooked egg from the base of the pan. When the eggs are almost ready, remove the pan from the heat and stir in the soy sauce. They will continue cooking in the residual heat from the pan. Serve immediately.

Also try

I like to add thinly sliced spring onions or chopped wild garlic leaves (if you can get hold of them) to the pan along with the tomatoes.

Courgette, marjoram and ricotta quiche

serves 4-6

For the pastry
160g plain flour
80g cold, unsalted butter
¼ tsp fine sea salt
1 egg yolk

For the filling
2 tbsp olive oil
2 banana shallots or 1 medium
    onion, sliced
2 cloves garlic, chopped
500g courgettes, halved and sliced
10g fresh marjoram, chopped
Zest of ½ lemon
250g ricotta
3 eggs
Sea salt and freshly ground black
    pepper

With crisp, buttery pastry and a deep, creamy filling full of savoury flavour, a well-made quiche can be one of the finest lunch dishes. Instead of the usual cream, this recipe uses ricotta, giving a lighter texture. A quiche is often best made in advance as it gives it time to set. This needs little adornment other than a simple green salad.

First make the pastry. Put the flour, butter and salt in a food processor and blitz for a few seconds, just enough to cut the butter into small chunks. Tip the mixture into a bowl and add the egg yolk. Using a fork, stir to distribute the yolk as best you can, before adding a little cold water, a tablespoon at a time, just until the mixture starts to come together. Use your hands to lightly press the dough to form it into a ball. The less you work the dough, the lighter the texture will be. Wrap the pastry in cling film and put it in the fridge to chill for at least 30 minutes.

Preheat the oven to 180°C/350°F/gas mark 4. On a floured surface roll out the pastry and line a 20cm tin with 4.5cm sides. Add a layer of baking parchment, fill the shell with baking beans and bake blind for 15 minutes. Remove the paper and beans and return the pastry shell to the oven for a further 15 minutes or until the pastry is lightly browned and the texture feels sandy. Remove from the oven and allow to cool while you make the filling.

Heat the oil in a heavy-bottomed pan with a lid and fry the shallots with a good pinch of salt over a medium heat for a few minutes until they start to soften. Add the garlic and continue to fry for a few more minutes before stirring in the courgettes and another good pinch of salt. Cover with the lid, and cook for about 5 minutes until the courgettes begin to soften. Remove the lid and cook for another 10-15 minutes, allowing them to colour slightly and become completely soft and sweet. Remove from the heat, add the marjoram and lemon zest and leave to cool slightly.

Whisk the ricotta in a large bowl, season well with salt and pepper and then whisk in the eggs.

Stir in the courgettes and then pour the mixture into the baked tart shell. Cook in the preheated oven 45 minutes, or until the top has puffed up slightly and browned and the centre feels just firm to the touch. Remove and cool a little before cutting.

Tomato and Gruyère quiche

serves 4-6

For the pastry
140g wholemeal flour
20g fine polenta flour or semolina
    flour
110g cold, unsalted butter
¼ tsp sea salt
1 egg yolk

For the roasted tomatoes
300g cherry tomatoes, halved
1 tsp sugar
1 tbsp mixed chopped fresh
    rosemary and thyme
1 tbsp olive oil
Sea salt and freshly ground black
    pepper

For the custard filling
250ml single cream
4 eggs, plus 1 egg yolk
180g Gruyère, grated
1 tbsp chopped fresh thyme
Sea salt and freshly ground black
    pepper

The slow-roasted tomatoes in this recipe are the sort of ingredient that always has a use in the kitchen. It's worth making double quantities to add them to tomato sauces, vegetable soups or stews, spread them on toast or stir into scrambled eggs. They will keep for about 3 days in the fridge.

I've used wholemeal pastry here - the nutty flavour of unrefined flour suits the acidity of the tomatoes in this quiche - and it can be used as an alternative wherever savoury pastry is called for. The addition of polenta flour gives the pastry an extra crunch, but can easily be replaced with an equal weight of wholemeal or plain flour.

_____

Put the flours in a food processor with the butter and salt. Blitz for a few seconds, just enough to cut the butter into small chunks but before the mixture resembles breadcrumbs.

Tip the mixture into a bowl and add the egg yolk. Using a fork, stir to distribute the yolk as best you can, before adding cold water, a tablespoon at a time, until the mixture starts to come together. Using your hands, gather up any loose flour and lightly press the pastry to form it into a ball. The less you work the dough, the better it will be.

Wrap in cling film and put it in the fridge to rest for at least 30 minutes.

While the dough is chilling, prepare the roasted tomatoes. Preheat the oven to 150°C/300°F/gas mark 2 and put the tomatoes in a roasting tin that fits them in a single layer. Sprinkle with the sugar, salt and pepper and the chopped herbs and then drizzle over the oil. Roast for 1 hour until they look a bit wrinkled and they taste sweet and intense.

On a floured surface, roll out the pastry. I like to use a high-sided 20cm tart tin but the quantities here will also suit a shallower 23cm tin. Line the tin with the pastry, pressing gently into the sides of the tin. Cover the pastry with a layer of baking parchment and fill the shell with baking beans. Bake blind in the preheated oven for 15 minutes then remove the paper and beans and return to the oven for a further 15 minutes. Allow to cool while you prepare the filling.

Increase the oven temperature to 200°C/400°F/gas mark 6.

Mix the cream, eggs, cheese and thyme in a large bowl and then stir in the roasted tomatoes. Taste and adjust the seasoning: remember if you plan to eat this cold, it will need more salt.

Pour the filling into the cooled shell and bake for 20-30 minutes (depending on depth of your tin). Test to see if it's done by pressing in the middle; it should feel slightly firm, with a little wobble and the sides should be puffed and browned. If not, return it to the oven for another 10 minutes.

Allow to cool slightly and continue to set before cutting.

Getting ahead
Both the tomatoes and the pastry can be prepared a day ahead; in fact a longer resting time in the fridge helps prevent the pastry from shrinking when cooked. Pastry also freezes well, either wrapped in cling film before rolling or once you have lined your tart tin (it can be baked from frozen). If you have frozen your pastry in a ball, simply defrost just enough to allow you to grate it straight into your tart tin. It can then be pressed into the base and sides of the tin by hand.

Omelette Arnold Bennett

serves 4–6

For the poached haddock
300g smoked haddock fillet
300ml milk
2 cloves
½ tsp peppercorns
1 bay leaf
Small bunch of parsley stalks
1 onion, thickly sliced
3 strips of lemon zest

For the béchamel
25g butter
20g plain flour
Zest of 1 lemon
1 tbsp finely chopped flat-leaf
    parsley
6 tarragon leaves, finely chopped
Sea salt and freshly ground black
    pepper

For the omelette
10g butter
6 eggs, lightly beaten
20g Parmesan, grated
Sea salt and freshly ground black
    pepper

This omelette is topped with a layer of juicy smoked haddock, covered in a delicately flavoured béchamel sauce and then finished under a hot grill The omelette that the writer Arnold Bennett asked the chef at the Savoy to make for him was prepared a little differently to this, but I'd like to thank him all the same for the inspiration.

––––––––––––––––––––––––

Cut the haddock fillet into three pieces so that it will fit comfortably in a medium pan. Pour over the milk and add the rest of the poaching ingredients. Bring to the boil and then simmer until cooked; this should take about 5–10 minutes, depending on the thickness of the fillet.

Remove the haddock with a slotted spoon and set aside. Strain the milk into a jug, discarding the solid remains.

Now make the sauce. Melt the butter in a pan over a medium heat, add the flour and cook for a minute so it starts to bubble and become slightly nutty. Pour the warm reserved milk in the pan and give it a good whisk. Bring it to the boil and cook for a minute, whisking, until it thickens to a smooth sauce.

Flake the poached haddock fillet and add to the sauce with the lemon zest and chopped herbs. Stir well and taste for seasoning - the haddock will be fairly salty but you will need to add some black pepper. (Up to this point, everything can be done in advance.)

Preheat the grill to its highest setting.

Melt the butter in a medium-sized omelette pan or ovenproof frying pan. Season the eggs with salt and pepper and when the butter is foaming, pour the eggs into the pan and tilt to cover the surface of the pan.

Agitate it lightly with a fork to move the eggs over the heat of the pan.

When it starts to set, lift up the sides, tilting the pan so the uncooked mixture flows underneath. The omelette will become gently ruckled.

When there is just a small amount of uncooked mixture on the top, remove from the heat.

Spread the haddock béchamel mixture over the top of the omelette and scatter over the grated Parmesan.

Place under the hot grill for 5–10 minutes, or until the cheese is melted and browned.

Italian egg drop soup

serves 2

600ml good-quality chicken stock
(or homemade cleared stock on
page 25)
Large handful of shredded spinach,
chard or kale
Shredded chicken pieces (optional)
2 eggs
30g grated Parmesan
Few gratings nutmeg
Zest of ¼ lemon
1 tbsp polenta flour
Sea salt and freshly ground black
pepper

Originally from Rome, this Italian egg soup (known as *stracciatella*) is traditionally eaten at Easter. Stracciatella means threads – in this case strands of cooked egg suspended in broth.

This method of enriching a broth with egg appears in many other guises too – the Japanese make egg drop soup by dropping beaten eggs into a broth of dashi, mirin and potato starch.

If you have cooked a roast chicken the bones can be used to make the stock and any shreds of cooked meat can be added too, providing extra substance.

_____

Put the chicken stock into a large pan and bring to the boil. Season well with salt and pepper. Add the greens and chicken pieces, if using, and cook for 1 minute until the leaves are tender.

In a small bowl, mix together the eggs, Parmesan, nutmeg, lemon zest and polenta flour to make a thick sauce.

Stir this into the stock and bring to the boil, cooking until the egg mixture solidifies into little streaks throughout the liquid. Serve hot.

Herb and potato frittata

serves 4-6

450g or about 3 medium potatoes,
　　such as Charlotte, Roosevelt or
　　another slightly waxy variety
15g butter
1 shallot, sliced
60g mixed herbs, such as parsley,
　　basil or marjoram, roughly
　　chopped
8 eggs, lightly beaten
Grating of nutmeg
1 tbsp olive oil
Sea salt and freshly ground black
　　pepper

You will need an ovenproof pan with a fairly small diameter (about 15-20cm). This will produce a lovely deep frittata which can be cut into thick slices. This is a good, quick dish to make if you have leftover cooked potatoes, and the method also works for a variety of alternative fillings (see below). A good frittata is never too crowded with ingredients, just keep the combinations simple.

_____

Preheat the oven to 200°C/400°F/gas mark 6.

Cut the potatoes into quarters lengthways, then into ½cm slices. Rinse the slices then cook in a large pan of boiling water for 6-8 minutes, or until tender. Drain and set aside to cool.

Melt the butter in the frying pan and add the chopped shallot and a little salt. Cook over a gentle heat for 5 minutes or so until soft but not coloured.

Put the chopped herbs in a bowl with the potatoes and shallots. Pour in the eggs and carefully stir to create a loose mixture. Grate over a little nutmeg and season well with salt and pepper. (If you plan to eat this cold, remember to add a bit more salt than you usually would.)

Heat the oil in the same pan that you cooked the shallots. When the oil is almost smoking hot, pour in the frittata mixture. Cook for about 5 minutes, to allow the bottom to get brown and set, then slide the pan into the preheated oven to cook the top. This should take about 15-20 minutes, depending on the thickness, but keep testing it by pressing the middle gently. It should feel just firm.

When it is done, remove from the oven and slide a palette knife around the edge to loosen it, before inverting it onto a plate.

Also try
The following fillings will also work:
· Sautéed courgettes, mint and ricotta
· Cooked spinach and herbs
· Cooked asparagus and Parmesan.

Thai-spiced Scotch eggs

makes 4

4 eggs
At least 1.5 litres sunflower oil,
   for frying

For the pork casing
400g minced pork or sausagemeat
1-2 stalks lemongrass, tough outer
   layers removed, finely chopped
4 lime leaves, finely chopped
1 small clove garlic, crushed to
   a paste with a pinch of salt
1 hot red chilli, seeded and finely
   chopped
2 tbsp soy sauce
Small bunch of coriander, finely
   chopped
1 tsp brown sugar or palm sugar
Sea salt and freshly ground black
   pepper

For the crumbed casing
40g plain flour, seasoned with salt
   and pepper
1 egg, beaten
Splash of milk
50g panko breadcrumbs

These are not as time-consuming to make as you might imagine and are infinitely more enjoyable for being home-made. Scotch eggs are the perfect picnic snack or packed lunch.

Quail's eggs could also be used if you wanted to create bite-sized canapés; just remember to reduce the quantities of casing (by about a third) and the cooking time for the eggs.

_____

Put the eggs in a pan and cover with cold water. Bring to the boil then turn down the heat and cook for 5 minutes. Refresh under cold water until cool enough to handle, then peel while still warm. Set aside.

Put all the ingredients for the pork casing into a large bowl and mix well with your hands. If you want to test or alter the seasonings at this stage, you can fry a teaspoonful of the mixture in a hot pan and then taste and adjust accordingly. Remember that the flavour will not be as strong when the mixture is cold.

To cover the eggs:
1. Take three shallow bowls and put the seasoned flour into one, the beaten egg mixed with milk in another and the breadcrumbs in a third. Next to the bowl of flour, put your cooked eggs.
2. Lay a sheet of baking parchment or cling film on top of a clean work surface and put the pork mixture onto it. Lay another sheet over the top and gently press to make a thin, flat disk. Peel off the top layer of paper.
3. Dip each cooked egg in flour and dust off any excess. Lay the eggs on the meat in an evenly spaced line and lift the bottom layer of paper to wrap the mixture over the top of the eggs, then peel the paper back to reveal the covered eggs.
4. Cut the meat into four (being careful not to slice through your egg). Dust your hands with flour and press the meat covered egg between your palms and form a round shape.
5. Lightly dust a covered egg with seasoned flour, then dip it into the beaten egg and finally coat in breadcrumbs.

Choose a pan that is deep enough for the eggs to be covered in the oil - I sometimes use a smaller pan and cook them one at a time, which requires less oil. Alternatively choose a larger pan and double the amount of oil - you may need up to 1.5 litres. (Any excess oil can be reused.)

Heat the oil until it reaches 170°C/340°F. If you don't have a thermometer, you can test the temperature but dropping in a scrap of bread; it should sizzle and turn golden immediately.

Using tongs or a slotted spoon, lower the eggs into the oil.

Fry for about 7 minutes so they are golden on the outside and the sausage meat is cooked through.

Remove to a plate then cover with kitchen paper and allow to cool slightly before eating.

These are best eaten warm but can be kept in the fridge for up to 3 days.

Also try
For vegetarian Scotch eggs, use leftover cooked risotto as the casing instead of the pork or sausagemeat, then coat in bread-crumbs as before.

Pink pickled eggs

makes 6

150ml cider vinegar
150ml red wine vinegar
200ml water
1 tbsp coriander seeds
1 tsp mustard seeds
½ tsp allspice berries
½ tsp black peppercorns
1 tsp fine sea salt
1 tbsp sugar
6 eggs
10g fresh tarragon
1 ready-cooked beetroot, peeled
  and sliced

These are not for the faint-hearted, although they are perhaps a little less intense than the ones you find at the bar in the pub. The colour that seeps from the beetroot makes them into something almost psychedelic when cut in half.

I like to eat these sliced in a salad with watercress and pieces of the pickled beetroot added too. They also look fabulous in a chopped egg sauce with their vibrant colour.

_____

First sterilise your jar and lid. Preheat the oven to 140°C/275°F/gas mark 1. Wash the jar in hot soapy water and rinse well. Place the jar and lid on a baking tray and put in the oven to dry completely (if you are using a jar with a rubber seal do not place the seal in the oven – simply wash thoroughly in hot water).

Put both vinegars in a pan with the water, spices, salt and sugar and bring to the boil. Remove from the heat and set aside.

Put the eggs into a pan large enough to hold them comfortably and cover with cold water. Bring to the boil and cook for 8 minutes. Drain and immediately cool under running water to prevent further cooking. Peel the eggs as soon as they are cool enough to handle.

Put the eggs, tarragon and beetroot slices into the sterilised jar and pour over the spiced vinegar. Seal and refrigerate for at least 3 days before eating. These pickled eggs can be kept for up to 3 months in the fridge.

TEA

Pistachio, apricot and orange blossom cake

serves 6-8

250g softened unsalted butter
250g sugar
Zest of ½ orange
2 tbsp orange blossom water
4 eggs (about 250g in weight)
100g ground pistachios
100g ground almonds
50g plain flour
1 tsp baking powder
Pinch fine sea salt
150g dried apricots, chopped

For the topping
50g sugar
Zest and juice of 1 lemon
3 tbsp chopped whole pistachios

Here the flavours of pistachio, apricot and orange blossom are inspired by sweet Arabic dishes. The ground nuts give the cake a dense, moist texture; it also helps it keep for longer.

_ _

Preheat the oven to 160°C/325°F/gas mark 3 and line a 900g loaf tin or 23cm round springform or loose-bottomed cake tin with baking parchment.

Beat the butter and sugar together using an electric stand mixer or handheld whisk until pale and fluffy. Add the orange zest and orange blossom water and mix well. Add the eggs one a time, mixing well after each addition, until completely incorporated. Add the ground nuts, flour, baking powder and salt and fold together with a metal spoon or spatula until you have a smooth batter. Finally, fold in the chopped apricots.

Pour into the prepared tin and bake in the preheated oven for 40 minutes.

Test to see if the cake is done by inserting a skewer into the middle; it should come out clean.

Allow to cool on a wire rack for 10 minutes before turning out.

While the cake is cooling, make the topping. Put the sugar in a small pan with the lemon zest and juice and bring to the boil. Add the chopped pistachios and stir well. Immediately pour over the top of the cake. Let it cool a little before cutting and serving.

Honey madeleines

makes 24

125g unsalted butter, plus extra
    for the tin
2 tbsp good-quality runny honey
3 eggs
120g caster sugar
125g self-raising flour, plus extra
    for the tin
Pinch sea salt

It's worth finding a madeleine tray, with its little scallop-shaped moulds, to create the unique madeleine shape. These cakes are wonderful to make with children: they are simple to prepare and taste best eaten immediately - good for those who can't wait.

————————————————————————

Melt the butter and honey together in a small pan.

In an electric stand mixer or using a handheld beater, whisk the eggs and sugar until they have doubled in volume and become thick enough that a dribble of mixture will leave a trail across the surface.

Pour the melted butter and honey into the eggs and whisk to combine.

Sift in the flour and salt and fold thoroughly with a metal spoon or spatula to combine and then chill for 1 hour.

Preheat the oven to 170°C/325°F/gas mark 3.

Melt about a tablespoon of butter and prepare a 12-hole madeleine tray by brushing the insides with the melted butter and dusting with a little flour.

Spoon half of the mixture into the moulds, but don't overfill as the cakes will rise. Keep the remaining mixture in the fridge to make the second batch.

Bake in the preheated oven for 12 minutes, or until risen and golden brown. Remove from the tin and repeat the process to cook the second batch.

Leave until just cool enough to handle - these are best eaten warm.

Also try
· Add lemon or orange zest to the batter.
· Add a few drops of almond extract instead of the honey.

Sweet popovers

makes 12

125g plain flour
3 tbsp icing sugar, plus extra to dust
Pinch sea salt
3 eggs
150ml milk
150ml cold water
1 tsp lightly ground fennel seeds,
    plus a few whole seeds to
    decorate
150g unsalted butter

These are basically a sort of sweet Yorkshire pudding: delicious 'puffs' of golden brown sweet batter, scented with fennel seed. Serve them straight from the oven while crisp and hot.

Preheat the oven to 220°C/425°F/gas mark 7.

Sift the flour, icing sugar and salt into a large bowl, making a well in the centre. Beat the eggs in a jug with the milk, water and ground fennel seeds and pour it gradually into the well, stirring to bring in the flour a little at a time. Keep adding the liquid and stirring until you have a smooth batter. Set aside to rest.

Put a 12-hole muffin tray into the oven to heat for a few minutes.

Melt the butter and pour about a tablespoon into each of the holes in the muffin tray followed by the batter.

Return to the oven and bake for 15-20 minutes, or until the tops look golden and have risen.

Remove from the oven, dust liberally with icing sugar and whole fennel seeds. Eat while still warm.

Also try
For a fruity version stir a spoonful of jam into the batter just before cooking.

Apple dragons

makes about 12

175g self-raising flour, plus extra
　　to dust
70g cold, unsalted butter, diced
35g sugar
¼ tsp ground cinnamon
Few gratings nutmeg
40g raisins
Pinch sea salt
1 eating apple (about 100g), peeled
　　and grated
1 egg, beaten
Butter, for frying
About 2 tbsp caster sugar, to dust

These little fried cakes are a derivative of Welsh cakes, (hence the name dragon, which is the symbol of Wales). The recipe uses grated apple to give them a softer texture and some natural sweetness.

This was a teatime favourite when I was a child – possibly because we lived very close to Wales, or perhaps because they are so easy to make with children. I like to sprinkle them with caster sugar when still hot to give them a crunchy texture – but of course you can use jam or honey instead.

––––––––––––––––––––––––

Sift the flour into a large bowl and add the butter. Use your fingertips to rub the butter into the flour until the mixture resembles coarse breadcrumbs (you can also do this in a food processor if you prefer).

Add the sugar, spices, raisins and salt and combine. Then add the grated apple and egg and bring the mixture together to a sticky-soft dough. Dust with extra flour if the mixture is too sticky then shape it into a disc, wrap in cling film and chill for 30 minutes.

Liberally sprinkle flour all over a clean work surface and lightly roll out the dough, coating in more flour if necessary, to a depth of barely 1cm. Using a 7cm pastry cutter or similar, cut out 12 circles, pressing any offcuts together and re-rolling.

Melt a little butter in a frying pan over a medium heat and gently fry the cakes for about 2–4 minutes on each side. They will expand slightly and get nice and brown.

Sprinkle with caster sugar while still hot and serve.

Marble genoise

serves 6-8

4 eggs
120g caster sugar
100g plain flour
10g cocoa powder
2 tbsp oil (sunflower, groundnut
 or grapeseed)
Pinch fine sea salt
1 tsp vanilla extract

A genoise sponge is one of the lightest of cakes. Only a small amount of flour is used and the well-whisked eggs fill the mixture with air. This looks most impressive baked in a loaf tin so that the dramatically contrasting cross section is visible when sliced.

Preheat the oven to 180°C/350°F/gas mark 4 and line a 21×6cm loaf tin with baking parchment.

Using an electric stand mixer or handheld whisk, beat the eggs and sugar until they are pale and thick and reach 'ribbon' consistency: when the beater or whisk is lifted the mixture should fall back onto the surface in a ribbon-like pattern that disappears after a few seconds. This will take 3-4 minutes with an electric whisk (longer if whisking by hand).

Divide the mixture (as equally as you can) between two bowls. Sift half the flour and all the cocoa powder into one bowl and fold to combine. Then fold in a tablespoon of the oil and a pinch of the salt.

Sift the rest of the flour into the other bowl and fold to combine. Add the other tablespoon of oil and the vanilla extract and fold a few more times so it is well mixed.

Pour a layer of cocoa mixture into the bottom of the prepared tin, then a layer of vanilla. Repeat until all the mixture is finished. Finally drag a knife or skewer through the mixture, along the length of the tin in a wiggly line.

It doesn't seem like much, but this is sufficient to create the marbled effect.

Bake in the preheated oven for 30 minutes, by which time the cake will have risen and a skewer inserted in the middle should come out clean. If not, return to the oven for another 5 minutes.

Transfer the tin to a wire rack to cool. When cool, run a knife around the edge and turn out.

Carrot cake

serves 6-8

3 eggs
100g caster sugar
70g soft brown sugar
1 tsp vanilla extract
1 tsp ground cinnamon
Few gratings nutmeg
Pinch ground cloves
5 carrots (about 350g), peeled and
    grated
100g pecan nuts, finely chopped
    (or use walnuts as an alternative)
200ml sunflower oil
190g plain flour, sifted
50g buckwheat flour
1 tsp baking powder
½ tsp bicarbonate of soda
Pinch fine sea salt

For the topping
150g unsalted butter, softened
300g soft cream cheese (preferably
    Philadelphia)
1 tsp vanilla extract
60g icing sugar

This cake has plenty of carrots in it, which makes it extra moist, and also means it keeps for longer. Using buckwheat flour gives the cake a delicious, nutty flavour but if you don't have any, you can replace it with the same amount of plain flour instead. I find most carrot cakes have an intensely sweet topping, so this recipe contains much less sugar, allowing the sweetness and flavour to come from the cake itself.

_____

Preheat the oven to 180°C/350°F/gas mark 4 and line a 30×20cm baking tin with baking parchment.

Beat the eggs and sugars together for about 5 minutes until light and creamy, either in an electric stand mixer or using a handheld electric whisk.

Add the vanilla extract, spices, grated carrots and nuts and mix together well.

Stir in the oil and then add the flours, baking powder, bicarbonate of soda and salt. Using a spatula or metal spoon, fold everything together gently but thoroughly.

Pour the mixture into the lined baking tin and bake for 45 minutes, or until a skewer inserted into the middle comes out clean. Leave to cool in the tin before turning out.

While the cake is cooling make the topping. Beat the butter until it becomes soft and creamy. Add the cream cheese and vanilla extract and beat together well before sifting in the icing sugar. Beat just enough to combine.

When the cake is cooled, spread a layer of topping over it and cut into squares to serve.

This cake will keep for at least 4 days wrapped in cling film so if you are not planning to eat it all in one go, only ice half the cake and keep the remainder of the icing in the fridge, covered in cling film until needed.

Brownies

makes about 24 small brownies

180g good-quality dark chocolate,
   minimum 70% cocoa solids
180g unsalted butter
1 tsp vanilla extract
200g caster sugar
Pinch fine sea salt
3 eggs, beaten
100g rice flour

A rich, intense, gooey brownie is a treat, until you have too much. By making a smaller batch, you'll never overdo it and it justifies spending money on the best ingredients (namely the chocolate). I also like to cut the brownies into smaller pieces, so a little goes a long way. Using rice flour makes these gluten free and gives them a softer texture, but if you don't have rice flour, plain flour can easily be substituted.

––––––––––––––––––––––––

Preheat the oven to 180°C/350°F/gas mark 4 and line a 30×20cm baking tin with baking parchment.

Place a large heatproof bowl over a pan of gently simmering water, making sure the base does not touch the water. Add the chocolate and butter to the bowl and heat until it melts.

Remove from the heat and add the vanilla extract, sugar and salt and whisk to combine.

Whisk in the eggs, then fold in the flour.

Pour the mixture into the lined tin and bake in the preheated oven for 15-20 minutes. The top should look pale and crackled when done while the middle should still feel soft when gently pressed. Don't forget that it will continue to cook in the residual heat from the tin when removed from the oven.

Allow to cool for about 15 minutes before removing from the tin and cutting into squares.

Also try
Add 150g chopped walnuts, hazelnuts, pecans, Brazil or macadamia nuts to the mixture.

Chocolate hazelnut salt crunch biscuits

makes about 12 biscuits

60g skinned hazelnuts
200g plain flour
½ tsp baking powder
½ tsp fine sea salt
90g caster sugar
80g soft light brown sugar
60g good-quality dark chocolate,
   minimum 70% cocoa solids
125g unsalted butter, melted
2 tbsp milk
1 tbsp vanilla extract
1 egg, beaten
Flaked sea salt, such as Maldon

Chocolate, hazelnut and salt are made for each other. This recipe makes a firm dough, which is easy to handle and has a crunchy texture when baked. These only take half and hour to make from start to finish, so they are great for a last-minute teatime treat.

———————————————————

Preheat the oven to 180°C/350°F/gas mark 4.

Spread the hazelnuts out onto a baking tray and toast in the oven for about 5-10 minutes, or until lightly golden. You can do this while the oven is warming up. Remove and cool slightly before chopping roughly.

Sift the flour, baking powder and fine salt into a large bowl and stir in the sugars. Slice the chocolate into rough shards, add to the flour with the chopped nuts and mix together.

Mix the melted butter, milk, vanilla extract and egg together and then pour into the dry ingredients. Mix briefly, just enough to bring the dough together.

Line a large baking sheet with baking parchment.

Put tablespoon-sized amounts of dough onto the lined baking sheet, leaving ample space around them so they have room to spread.

Sprinkle a little flaked sea salt over each and bake in the preheated oven for 12 minutes. They should be browned all over. Remove and transfer to a wire rack to cool.

———————————————————

Note: The dough can be made a day or two in advance - just wrap in cling film and chill until needed.

Rich chocolate, almond and orange cake

A wonderfully rich and intense chocolate cake, loosely inspired by the dense Sachertorte from Vienna. It looks very elegant as a birthday cake covered in candles, or it could be served as a dessert, with a spoonful of crème fraîche or the zabaglione ice cream on page 181.

----

serves 6-8

85g good-quality dark chocolate, minimum 70% cocoa solids
120g unsalted butter
120g caster sugar
2 pinches ground cinnamon
2 pinches ground allspice
1 tsp vanilla extract
Zest of ½ orange
3 eggs
2 tbsp milk
150g ground almonds
60g plain flour
½ tsp baking powder

For the glaze
80g dark chocolate, minimum 70% cocoa solids
1 tbsp sugar
20g unsalted butter
4 tbsp orange marmalade

Preheat the oven to 180°C/350°F/gas mark 4 and butter and line a 23cm round springform or loose-bottomed cake tin.

Place a heatproof bowl over a pan of gently simmering water, making sure the base of the bowl is just above the water. Add the chocolate to the bowl and heat until it melts completely.

Put the butter, sugar, spices, vanilla extract and orange zest in a separate large bowl and beat until light and fluffy, using an electric whisk if you have one. Beat in the eggs, one at a time, and then the milk and ground almonds, followed by the melted chocolate. Sift in the flour and baking powder and gently fold everything together.

Pour into the prepared tin and bake in the preheated oven for 30 minutes. Test to see if the cake is done by inserting a skewer into the middle; it should come out clean. Allow to cool completely before turning out onto a wire rack.

To make the glaze, put the chocolate, sugar, butter and 2 table-spoons of water in a pan and melt very gently over a low heat. It should become smooth with a loose, pouring consistency. If not, add a little more water.

Put the marmalade in a separate pan with a tablespoon of water and bring to the boil. Pour through a sieve to remove the pieces of rind, so you are left with a smooth jelly.

Spread a layer of the marmalade over the top of the cake, then pour or spread the chocolate glaze over the top, letting it dribble down the sides. Use a palette knife to then smooth it over the cake and around the sides.

Pistachio and apricot meringues

makes about 12

6 medium egg whites (about 210g)
Pinch fine sea salt
420g caster sugar (or double the
   weight of the whites, see above)
4 tbsp chopped dried apricots
4 tbsp chopped or ground
   pistachios

Everyone needs to have a meringue recipe up their sleeve: the rule to remember is to use double the weight of sugar to whites. So if one egg white weighs 35g, use 70g sugar. Meringues are best made in an electric stand mixer, so you can get the whites really well whisked. You can, of course, whisk by hand; you just need to be patient and strong. See page 8 for advice on storing and whisking egg whites.

Once you've mastered the basics of meringue, you can make any variety - large, small, studded with chocolate or bright with zest.

Preheat the oven to 110°C/220°F/gas mark ¼ and line a baking sheet with baking parchment.

Using an electric handheld whisk or stand mixer, whisk the egg whites until they form soft peaks. Continue whisking, adding the salt and a few large spoonfuls of sugar at a time, making sure it's incorporated before you add the next bit. The mixture should start to become silky and thick. When it's all incorporated, keep mixing for a few more minutes until it is glossy, thick and stands in stiff peaks.

Fold the chopped apricots and pistachios into the mixture.

Use a large spoon to scoop dollops of the mixture onto the paper, leaving a few centimetres between each one so they have room when they expand in the oven. For a final flourish, use the back of the spoon in a circular motion to smooth out the mixture, lifting the spoon at the end to make a little point in the centre.

Bake for 1-1½ hours, or until dry and crisp and easy to lift off the paper.

Also try
Other meringue variations include:
- Folding slivers of bitter chocolate or a mixture of orange and lemon zest into the meringues before cooking
- Making plain meringues and serving with chestnut purée and whipped cream and melted chocolate poured over the top.

Seville orange tartlets

makes 6-8

For the pastry
140g wholemeal flour
20g fine polenta flour
100g cold, unsalted butter
Pinch fine sea salt
4 tbsp icing sugar
1 egg yolk

For the curd
225g caster sugar
Juice of 3 Seville oranges, plus the zest of ½ of one of them
5 egg yolks
300g cold unsalted butter, cut into cubes

50g candied peel, roughly chopped (optional)

These little tarts are pretty and elegant to eat at teatime. Not all tart fillings suit this sweet wholemeal pastry but here the richness and tang of the curd goes beautifully with the earthy, crunchy pastry - it feels like a sophisticated version of marmalade on toast.

Seville oranges have a relatively short season but it is wonderful to have a chance to use them (especially if you don't make marmalade) and they are now quite easy to buy in supermarkets. However, lemon curd can always be used as an alternative (see page 114).

I sometimes use individual loose-bottomed tart tins but if you don't have these, use a muffin tray to make individual pastry cups.

Put both flours in a food processor with the butter, salt and icing sugar. Blitz for a few seconds, just until the mixture becomes like coarse breadcrumbs. Alternatively, sift the flours, salt and sugar into a large bowl and use your fingertips to rub in the butter.

Pour the mixture into a bowl and add the egg yolk. Using a fork, stir to distribute the yolk as best you can, before adding a little cold water, a tablespoon at a time, until the mixture starts to come together. Using your hands, gather up any loose flour and lightly press the pastry to form it into a ball. The less you work the dough, the better it will be.

Wrap in cling film and put it in the fridge to rest for at least 30 minutes.

Roll the pastry out on a lightly floured surface and cut out circles large enough to line your individual tart shells or muffin tray holes. If using a muffin tray, the pastry only needs to come halfway up the sides. Lightly press the pastry into the moulds, leaving the edges a big ragged if you wish. Chill in the fridge for 20 minutes.

Preheat the oven to 150°C/300°F/gas mark 2.

Line each pastry shell with baking parchment and fill with baking beans. Bake in the preheated oven for 10 minutes, then remove the paper and baking beans and cook for a further 10 minutes, or until just browned. Allow to cool.

Meanwhile make the curd. Put the sugar, juice, zest and egg yolks together in a pan over a low heat and warm gently, stirring. Start adding the butter, a few cubes at a time, stirring continuously until the mixture starts to thicken. When all the butter is incorporated the mixture should be smooth and thick. Be careful not to overheat or the eggs will scramble. Strain to remove the zest, which would give the tartlets a bitter taste.

Fill the cooled pastry shells with the warm curd and leave to cool and set completely. Sprinkle each one with a little candied peel, if using, and serve.

Lemon curd

makes 550g curd (or enough to fill
a 23cm tart shell)

225g caster sugar
Zest and juice of 3 lemons
5 egg yolks
300g cold unsalted butter, cut into
cubes

Lemon curd is a teatime classic and is delicious on scones
or toasted brioche (see page 48) or as a filling for sponge
cakes and biscuits. However, it also has many uses in popular
desserts, such as a base for lemon meringue tart or a filling
for profiteroles (see page 172). Look out for Amalfi lemons for
the best flavour.

Put the sugar, lemon zest and juice and egg yolks together in
a pan over a low heat and warm gently, stirring occasionally.

Start adding the butter, a few cubes at a time, stirring continuously until the mixture starts to thicken. When all the butter
is incorporated the mixture should be smooth and thick. Be
careful not to overheat or the eggs will scramble. Strain to
remove the zest and allow to cool slightly before using.

Fresh lemon curd can be kept for up to 3 days in the fridge in
an airtight container.

Teatime crêpes

makes 10-12 crêpes, serving 4-6

120g plain flour
Pinch fine sea salt
200ml milk
100ml water
2 eggs
20g unsalted butter, plus extra
    for frying
Lemon wedges, to serve
Caster sugar, to serve

The secret to lacy crêpes is the thinnest batter and a very hot pan. When the batter is poured into the pan, it will spread easily to form a delicate film. It's also helpful to let the batter rest for at least half an hour if you can; if you want you could make it the day before. Just give it a good stir before using, adding a little water if it has thickened slightly.

Good crêpes are best served simply - just a squeeze of fresh lemon juice and a sprinkle of caster sugar.

Sift the flour into a bowl and add the salt. Put the milk, water and eggs into a jug and whisk well.

Make a well in the middle of the flour and pour in the milk mixture, a little at a time, stirring with a wooden spoon to gradually bring the flour in from the sides until you have a smooth batter. Pour the batter back into the jug and leave to rest for at least 30 minutes.

Melt the butter in the frying pan you are going to use to cook the crêpes, then pour it into the batter. Give the batter a good stir, it should have the consistency of single cream. If not, add a little more water. The pan will now have a good film of butter in it for you to cook your first crêpe.

Make sure the pan is really hot and pour a small amount of batter from the jug into the pan, tilting it all around as you go so that the batter spreads in a very thin layer over the bottom. Any extra batter you can pour back into the jug.

Cook for a minute or so until small bubbles appear on the surface and then use a spatula to gently ease the sides of the crêpe away from the pan. Carefully turn and cook for another minute on the other side.

Use a piece of kitchen paper to rub a tiny bit more butter into the pan before cooking each crêpe.

Crêpes can be made in advance and reheated easily. Just stack the cooked crepes on top of each other and cover with baking parchment or cling film and store in the fridge until needed. To reheat, put them in a low oven or heat individually in a frying pan with some butter.

SUPPER

Spinach, marjoram and ricotta sformata

Sformata is an Italian dish, similar to a soufflé or rather like a baked flan but without the pastry shell – the word *sformata* means misshapen! Leafy greens like spinach or chard have a real affinity with the soft, fragrant taste of marjoram or oregano.

----

serves 4

1 tsp unsalted butter, plus extra
    to butter the dish
50g Parmesan, grated
500g spinach, washed and large
    stalks removed
300g ricotta
6 eggs
300g crème fraîche
Few gratings nutmeg
2 tbsp chopped fresh marjoram
Sea salt and freshly ground black
    pepper

Preheat the oven to 200°C/400°F/gas mark 6. Butter an oval 30×20cm ovenproof baking dish and dust all over with a tablespoon of the grated Parmesan.

Melt the teaspoon of butter in a large, lidded pan and throw in the spinach with just the water clinging to its leaves. Season with salt and pepper, stir briefly then put on a lid so it steams and wilts, this should take about 2 minutes.

Tip the cooked spinach into a sieve and squeeze any excess moisture out, before chopping roughly.

In a bowl, whisk the ricotta to break up any lumps, add the eggs and continue whisking so that bubbles form. Stir in the crème fraîche, nutmeg, marjoram and remaining Parmesan. Finally stir in the chopped spinach and pour into the prepared dish.

Bake in the preheated for 25 minutes or until the top is slightly risen and browned and the centre of the sformata feels slightly firm to the touch.

Vegetables 'à la Grecque' with chopped egg and herb sauce

Poaching vegetables 'à la Grecque' is a when a poaching liquor, made from wine, lemon, coriander seeds and other spices, is used to infuse the vegetables with a delicate and fragrant flavour. This is a lovely dish to make when spring produce arrives, especially asparagus and baby leeks, which taste particularly good with the egg sauce. For a more substantial meal, serve with poached chicken or some simply cooked fish. Or for an easy and refreshing summer lunch, cook in advance and serve cold - once prepared, it will keep happily for 24 hours in the fridge.

_____

serves 4

4 eggs
2 tbsp small capers, rinsed
1 tbsp Dijon mustard
1 tbsp good red wine vinegar
Bunch (20g) of flat-leaf parsley, finely chopped
Bunch (20g) of basil, finely chopped
4-6 tbsp extra-virgin olive oil, plus extra to serve
8 baby leeks, well washed
3 carrots, peeled
4 celery sticks (preferably the tender ones near the heart)
Small bunch of asparagus
½ cauliflower
Sea salt and freshly ground black pepper

For the poaching liquor
Juice of ½ lemon
100ml white wine
1 tsp coriander seeds
½ tsp peppercorns
1 bay leaf
Sprig of thyme
Few fennel fronds or parsley stalks

To make the sauce, hard-boil the eggs for 12 minutes, then drain and run under cold water to cool before peeling.

Roughly chop the capers and put them in a bowl with the mustard, vinegar, parsley, basil and oil.

Grate or finely chop the eggs and add to the bowl, mixing well to make a sauce. Season to taste.

Prepare the vegetables so they are roughly the same size: slice the leeks and carrots lengthways in half and the celery into similar lengths; break the cauliflower into florets.

Put all the ingredients for the poaching liquor into a large pan and add a litre of water and a teaspoon of salt. Bring to the boil then add the leeks. After a minute add the other vegetables and gently simmer for 3 minutes, or until the vegetables feel tender but still have a little bite. Remove with a slotted spoon and transfer to a serving dish. Pour over a spoonful of the poaching liquid, season and dress with a little olive oil.

Add another spoonful of the poaching liquid to the egg sauce and stir to loosen it slightly. Serve the warm vegetables with the sauce spooned over the top.

Ouefs en meurette

serves 4

400ml red wine
400ml good-quality chicken stock
4 eggs
200g button mushrooms
70g pancetta, cut into cubes
  or lardons
1 shallot, sliced
Few sprigs of thyme
2 bay leaves
50g unsalted butter
1 tbsp olive oil
4 slices of toast
1 tbsp plain flour
1 tbsp freshly chopped flat-leaf
  parsley
Sea salt and freshly ground black
  pepper

This dish originates from the Burgundy region of France, where it is made with the local wine. The eggs are poached in wine to give them a beautiful purple colour and the wine is then reduced to make a sauce, enriched with butter. It's a dish which tastes as good as the quality of its ingredients, so do try to use the best wine you can. I make this when I've got any leftovers from a good bottle. This recipe does have a few steps, but much of it can be made in advance.

————————————————

Put the wine and stock in a pan and bring to a simmer. Carefully slide the eggs into the pan and poach them for 3 minutes so that the yolks are still runny. Transfer to a plate with a little of the poaching liquid, cover and keep warm. (A bowl set over hot water is a good trick, or put them in the oven at a very low temperature.)

Remove the stalks from the mushrooms and save the caps for later. Add the mushroom stalks, a couple of the pancetta cubes, the shallot and herbs to the pan of poaching liquid. Bring to the boil and cook to reduce to approximately 200ml. This will take about 10-15 minutes.

In the meantime, place a frying pan over a medium heat, melt a small knob of the butter and fry the rest of the pancetta until it starts to crisp, then remove and set aside.

Cut the mushroom caps into quarters, then melt another knob of butter in the same pan and add the mushrooms. Season well with salt and pepper and fry until soft and coloured all over.

When the stock and wine are sufficiently reduced, strain and discard all the solids. Taste and adjust the seasoning.

Using the same frying pan, which will now have all the delicious flavours of the cooked bacon and mushrooms in it, melt another knob of the butter and add the oil. Fry the toasted bread on each side so it absorbs all the flavours of the pan. Remove and keep warm.

To finish the sauce, melt the rest of the butter in the frying pan and stir in the flour. Cook, stirring, for a minute; the flour will brown slightly and give off a nutty aroma. Pour the reduced wine into the pan and let it boil, stirring to produce a smooth, slightly thickened sauce. Add the cooked pancetta and mushrooms and stir together. Up to this point, everything can be done in advance and kept warm.

To serve, lay an egg on each piece of toast and pour the sauce over the top, distributing the pancetta and mushrooms evenly over each. Sprinkle with chopped parsley.

Omelette fines herbes

serves 2

4 eggs
2 tbsp chopped flat-leaf parsley
1 tbsp chopped chervil (optional)
4-6 tarragon leaves, chopped (use
    fewer leaves if you're using
    chervil too)
1 tbsp chopped chives
20g unsalted butter
Sea salt and freshly ground black
    pepper

An omelette is a beautiful, simple thing, even in its plainest form. Other ingredients can make delicious embellishments but as the famous cookery writer Margaret Costa wisely said, these should be added with 'discretion and economy'. Omelette fines herbes is a classic French omelette that really allows the flavour of fresh herbs to shine (dried herbs are no substitute here). The key is to use the correct size of pan: a 23cm skillet will give you right thickness when cooking the omelettes one at a time.

————————————————————————

Crack the eggs into a bowl and add the chopped herbs, salt and pepper and a small knob of the butter. Lightly beat with a fork.

Place a 23cm skillet or frying pan over a high heat and melt half the remaining butter in it, swirling so it covers the whole surface and the sides.

Using a ladle, pour half the egg mixture into the pan and tilt to cover the whole surface. Use a fork to 'agitate' the eggs and circulate the heat from the bottom of the pan.

When the omelette starts to set, use the edge of the fork to lift up the sides of the omelette, tilting the pan so the uncooked mixture can flow underneath. The surface will become gently ruckled.

When there is just a small amount of uncooked mixture on the top, fold the omelette in three and cook for a few more seconds before sliding onto a warm plate.

Repeat to make the second omelette.

Also try
Omit the herbs from this recipe and add any of the following fillings before folding the omelette:
· Shredded sorrel or chopped fresh herbs
· Sautéed mushrooms
· Fresh crabmeat
· Chopped tomatoes and basil

Oeufs en gelée

makes 6

1 tbsp light flavoured oil for
greasing (grapeseed, groundnut
or light olive oil work well)
9 sheets leaf gelatine
1 tbsp vermouth, dry sherry or
white wine
600ml homemade cleared chicken
stock (page 25)
Couple of slices of cooked ham,
cut into strips
Few tarragon leaves
4 *mollet* (soft-boiled) eggs, peeled
Sea salt and freshly ground black
pepper

This classic hors d'oeuvre can be a bit of a palaver to make,
especially if you are cooking the stock from scratch. However,
these wobbly, translucent cases of jelly, with an egg suspended
inside, are such a joy to behold on the plate it will all seem
worth it. The fresher your eggs, the harder they are to peel, so
this is not a recipe that calls for eggs fresh from the nest. Here
you want perfectly smooth whites visible through the
translucent jelly.

You need individual moulds which are large enough to hold a
whole egg with some space around it – improvise with dariole
moulds, large coffee cups or any little oval moulds.

————————————————

Brush the insides of four moulds with oil.

Pour cold water over the leaf gelatine and soak for 5 minutes,
or until soft and floppy.

Stir the vermouth, sherry or white wine into the cold stock
and season well with salt and pepper.

Remove the gelatine sheets from the water and put them in
a pan. Place over a low heat for a few seconds, just so they start
to melt. Pour the stock into the pan and mix well to disperse
the dissolved gelatine.

Coil a strip of ham around the inside each mould and lay a
couple of tarragon leaves on the base.

Pour about 1cm of the aspic (the gelatine and stock mixture)
into the bottom of each mould and put in the freezer for 5-10
minutes to set.

Remove from the freezer and place a *mollet* egg (see page 14)
into each mould, on top of the layer of the set aspic and pour
over the remaining liquid aspic to cover. Add a few more
tarragon leaves to each mould, then cover and leave to set
in the fridge for at least 5 hours.

The aspic can be kept in the fridge for up to 3 days, but remember, the longer it chills, the more set it will become.

Cheese soufflé

serves 4

35g unsalted butter
110g mixed grated cheese
    (Parmesan, Gruyère or pecorino
    all work well)
250ml milk
½ tsp cayenne
Few gratings nutmeg
1 tbsp plain flour
4 egg yolks
5 egg whites
Sea salt and freshly ground black
    pepper

One of the most surprising things about cheese soufflé is how easy it is to make. I often cook it for a Sunday night or emergency supper dish when I haven't got time to shop - cheese, eggs and milk are usually always in my fridge. Served with a green salad with a mustardy dressing, it provides the perfect meal. There's no need to be scared of soufflés, especially one like this, which will still taste delicious even if it barely rises.

Preheat the oven to 200°C/400°F/gas mark 6.

Melt 10g of the butter and brush it all over the surface of a deep 25cm oval or square ovenproof dish. Dust with 10g of the grated cheese.

Put the milk in a pan with a good pinch of salt, some pepper, the cayenne and a few gratings of nutmeg. Bring to the boil and then immediately remove from the heat.

In a separate pan, melt the remaining butter and add the flour. Cook, stirring, for a minute so it starts to foam but not brown. Pour in all the hot milk and whisk well. Bring to the boil and cook for another minute, stirring continuously. The mixture will thicken slightly.

Pour the mixture into a large bowl and whisk in the egg yolks and the remaining grated cheese.

Whisk the egg whites with a pinch of salt until stiff peaks form. Add a good spoonful of egg white into the cheese mixture and stir to loosen it slightly.

Gently fold the rest of the whites into the mixture until thoroughly incorporated. Pour into the soufflé dish and bake in the preheated oven for 25 minutes.

To test to see if the soufflé is done, gently press the top; it should be soft and springy. Remove from the oven and serve immediately while it is nicely risen.

Tip: rather that using a pan to melt the butter for the soufflé dish, I just put the knob of butter in the dish and put it in the hot oven for a minute, then use a pastry brush to brush all over the surface.

Also try
Experiment with other ingredients stirred into the egg yolk base with the cheese - spinach, puréed asparagus, smoked haddock or ham are all delicious alternatives.

Tagliatelle with asparagus and fonduta sauce

serves 4

½ clove garlic
4 egg yolks
200g crème fraîche
100g Parmesan, grated, plus extra
   to serve
200g asparagus spears, sliced on
   the diagonal into 2cm lengths
1 quantity of rich pasta dough
   (see page 20), cut into tagliatelle
   ribbons, or about 300g fresh
   tagliatelle pasta
Sea salt and freshly ground black
   pepper

This is one of my favourite ways to eat asparagus: stirred through rich, silky pasta and smothered in a creamy, savoury fonduta custard, made with Parmesan and crème fraîche.

_____

Bring a pan of water to a gentle simmer. Rub the inside of a heatproof bowl with the cut side of the garlic. Add the egg yolks, crème fraîche and Parmesan to the bowl and season well. Whisk the mixture together well and then set the bowl over the pan without the base touching the water.

Continue to whisk as the mixture heats. At first it will become quite liquid, then as the heat builds and the yolks cook, the mixture will begin to thicken. This can take up to 10 minutes. The end consistency should be like very thick cream.

Remove the fonduta from the heat so it doesn't carry on cooking.

In a large pan of boiling, salted water, cook the asparagus and the pasta together for 2-3 minutes or until al dente.

Drain, reserving about 100ml of the cooking water. Pour the fonduta mixture over the pasta and asparagus and season well with salt and pepper. Toss everything together, adding enough of the reserved cooking water to create a creamy sauce. Sprinkle with extra Parmesan to serve.

Also try
Use peas and broad beans instead of asparagus with some crispy fried pancetta strips sprinkled on top.

Kamut pasta with bottarga and celery

Bottarga di muggine is cured grey mullet roe. It has a waxy texture and a unique savoury, buttery, fishy flavour. It's available from good Italian grocery stores or online, and like many good-quality ingredients, it can be expensive. However, a little goes a long way and it keeps well for several weeks if stored in the fridge. Try to buy the bottarga as a whole piece, rather than pre-grated.

----

serves 4

100g bottarga
Juice of ½ lemon
4 tbsp extra-virgin olive oil, plus extra to serve
1 tbsp olive oil, for frying
6 celery sticks, finely sliced
Pinch dried chilli flakes
1 quantity of Kamut pasta (see page 24), cut into thin ribbons (tagliarini), or about 300g dried pasta
Sea salt and freshly ground black pepper

Grate the bottarga into a bowl and mix in the lemon juice; it will dissolve into a thick sauce. Add the extra-virgin olive oil, a little at a time, stirring to make an emulsion. Season with black pepper.

In a frying pan, heat the oil for frying over a medium heat and add the sliced celery with a good pinch of salt and the chilli flakes. Fry for a few minutes until soft and slightly browned.

Cook the pasta in plenty of boiling salted water for 3 minutes. Drain, keeping about 50ml of the cooking water to add later. Return the cooked pasta back to the empty pan.

Stir a few tablespoons of the cooking water into the bottarga sauce and then pour over the pasta. Add the celery and season well with salt and pepper. Toss to coat all the ribbons and add more of the cooking water if it looks a little dry.

Serve with a little extra-virgin olive oil poured over the top.

Baked eggs with sweetcorn, chilli and cheese

Sweetcorn, chilli and cheese is a favourite combination of mine and the slight crunch of the corn contrasts well with the soft egg, suspended in its creamy sauce. You can make these individually in ramekins, or increase the quantities and make several servings in one larger ovenproof dish, just remember it will take a little longer to cook.

————————————————————

serves 2

20g butter, plus extra for greasing
4 tbsp fresh sweetcorn (about 1 small cob), although good tinned sweetcorn can be used instead
1 clove garlic, halved lengthways
2 eggs
2 tbsp crème fraîche or sour cream
2 tbsp chipotle chilli sauce (if you don't have chipotle, use another chilli sauce or pinch dried chilli flakes)
4 tbsp grated Parmesan or pecorino
Sea salt and freshly ground black pepper

Preheat the oven to 200°C/400°F/gas mark 6.

Shave the sweetcorn kernels from the cob with a sharp knife.

Melt a little butter in a pan and add the sweetcorn. Season well and sauté for a minute before adding just enough water to almost cover it. Let the water bubble and reduce until it has almost all evaporated. The corn will be tender, but still have a little bite.

Rub the insides of two ramekins or small ovenproof dishes with the cut side of the garlic clove and a little butter.

Divide the corn equally between the ramekins, make an indentation in the middle of each and break an egg over the top, so the yolk sits in the hole with the white spilling over it. Put a dollop of crème fraîche on top on each egg, season well, then add the chilli sauce. Finally sprinkle grated cheese on top.

Put the ramekins in a baking tray and pour boiling water (from the kettle) into the tray to come halfway up the sides of the ramekins.

Bake for 15 minutes, or until the top is browned and the egg feels just firm when pressed. The yolk should be runny inside. If you prefer the yolk more cooked, return to the oven for a further 5 minutes.

Squash gnocchi

serves 6

500g squash (onion, crown prince
  or butternut are good varieties to
  use, the more floury, the better),
  peeled and seeds removed
2 tbsp olive oil
few pinches dried chilli flakes
2 tbsp fresh oregano
375g floury potatoes (about 2-3),
  peeled
Few gratings nutmeg
1-2 eggs
150g good-quality plain flour, plus
  extra for rolling
50g butter
Parmesan, to serve
Sea salt and freshly ground black
  pepper

Homemade gnocchi has such a light and delicate texture compared to the commercially produced semolina variety. Even if you just try making this once, it's worth it to see how such simple ingredients - egg, potato and squash - can combine to become such a special dish.

— —

Preheat the oven to 220°C/425°F/gas mark 7.

Cut the squash into slim wedges and toss in a baking tray with the olive oil, chilli flakes, half the oregano and some salt and pepper. Roast in the oven for 15-20 minutes, or until completely soft and cooked through.

Meanwhile, boil the potatoes in plenty of salted water until they are completely soft. Drain and mash. If you have a potato ricer, this is definitely the time to use it as the smoother the mash, the better.

Mash the roasted squash and gently stir together with the potato. Season well with salt and pepper and a little nutmeg. Beat the eggs and add them to the mixture a little at a time. You don't want the mixture to become too sloppy and you can always add more egg later so take care at this stage. Add most of the flour and beat briskly to create a soft, sticky dough, the texture of a thick cake mix. Taste and adjust the seasoning as necessary.

Liberally dust a work surface and your hands with flour. Take a large tablespoon of the mixture, drop it onto the prepared surface and lightly roll it around in the flour until it is well coated. This will make it easier to handle.

Gently roll it with your palms into a long sausage shape before cutting it into short lengths. Repeat with the rest of the mixture.

Bring a large pan of water to the boil and add a good pinch of salt. Drop the gnocchi into the water and simmer for about 3 minutes. Initially the gnocchi will sink but as soon as they are cooked, they will float to the surface. When this happens scoop them out with a slotted spoon.

To serve, melt the butter in a pan with the remaining oregano until the butter just begins to brown. Pour the melted butter and oregano all over the gnocchi and sprinkle with grated Parmesan cheese.

Lentil curry with eggs

serves 4-6

400g brown lentils
30g fresh ginger, peeled
4 cloves garlic
2 red chillies, stalks removed
1 onion, roughly chopped
1 tsp sea salt
2 tbsp vegetable oil
4 tomatoes, skinned, seeded and
    chopped (you could also use
    tinned peeled plum tomatoes,
    drained, seeded and chopped)
4 hard-boiled eggs, peeled
20g fresh coriander, roughly
    chopped
4 tbsp natural yoghurt

For the spice mix
1 tsp cardamom pods
6 cloves
3 tsp cumin seeds
2 tsp ground turmeric
2 bay leaves
1 cinnamon stick

Eggs seem to have a natural affinity with the aromatic flavours of spices and chilli heat. It's no wonder they are often found in recipes with curried sauces. This meat-free dish provides all the protein you need. Not only is it spicy and filling, it can also be put together in no time.

————————————————————

Put the lentils into a large pan, cover with cold water and bring to the boil. Reduce the heat to a simmer and leave to cook for 15-20 minutes, or until tender, topping up the water if needed.

Meanwhile, make the spice mix. Place a large frying pan, without any oil, over a medium heat and add the cardamom pods, cloves and cumin seeds. After about 30 seconds they should start to give off a toasted, fragrant aroma. Shake the pan gently and cook for another 30 seconds then immediately remove from the heat and grind in a pestle and mortar or spice grinder. Once partially ground, you can remove and discard the papery husks of the cardamom, releasing the black seeds inside. Continue grinding until you have a coarse powder. Add the turmeric, bay leaves and cinnamon stick and set aside.

Put the ginger, garlic, whole chillies, onion and salt into a food processor and blitz to make a paste.

Return the frying pan to the heat and add the oil. When it is hot, add the paste and fry over a medium heat for a few minutes. Then add the spice mix and the tomatoes and cook on a low heat for another 5 minutes or so.

When the lentils are tender, strain them to remove any excess liquid (reserving the liquid) and return the lentils to the pan. Add all the aromatic spice mixture and the boiled eggs to the pan and stir well. If the mixture looks too dry add some of the reserved liquid to make a loose sauce.

Cook the lentils for another 5 minutes so they become infused with the spice flavours. (Up to this point, everything can be done in advance and reheated when needed.)

When you're ready to serve, sprinkle with the chopped coriander and stir in the yoghurt to make a creamy sauce surrounding the lentils and eggs. This is delicious on its own although you could serve with some sautéed spinach and steamed basmati rice.

Chopped egg on toast with cod's roe and crème fraîche

serves 2

1 hard-boiled egg, finely chopped
1 tsp salted capers, rinsed, drained
   and finely chopped
2 spring onions, finely chopped
1 tsp soft unsalted butter
2 tbsp cod's roe (or other fish roe)
2 slices of toast
2 tsp crème fraîche
Sea salt and freshly ground black
   pepper

This is a lovely light supper but could also be served as a starter, or something to eat with drinks. Crème fraîche and fish eggs both last well in the fridge so it's great as a standby dish.

If you can't find cod's roe, smoked herring or salmon roe are good alternatives.

_____

Mix the egg, capers, spring onions and butter together and season with salt and pepper.

Spread both the mixture and then a tablespoon of cod's roe over each slice of hot toast. Top with crème fraiche.

Chicken 'n' egg – a Japanese dish

serves 2

150g dried rice (basmati, brown rice or Japanese-style short grain)
200ml good-quality chicken stock (preferably cleared chicken stock, page 25)
1 tbsp soy sauce
1 tsp sugar
200g chicken breasts, sliced into finger-sized pieces (or leftover cooked chicken torn into strips)
3 spring onions, sliced
2 eggs, stirred to break up the yolk, not beaten

This is great comfort food and makes a perfect quick supper. In Japan, sticky short grain rice is used, but you could eat this with basmati, brown rice or omit the rice altogether and use wilted greens instead.

I love to make this when I have any leftover roast chicken or homemade stock in the fridge.

_____

Cook the rice according to the packet instructions. Drain and keep warm.

Put the stock into a deep pan and bring to the boil. Add the soy sauce and sugar and stir well to dissolve the sugar.

Add the sliced chicken and spring onion to the stock and reduce the heat to a simmer. Cook for 3-5 minutes or until the chicken is no longer pink.

Pour in the eggs and turn up the heat. They will bubble up around the edges of the pan, forming soft curds. Turn down the heat to a gentle simmer and let the eggs cook for a minute.

Spoon the rice into two bowls and add the chicken, onions and egg. Pour a few ladles of stock over each bowl and serve.

Skate wings with sauce gribiche

Gribiche is essentially a flavoured mayonnaise made using cooked instead of raw egg yolks. The capers, cornichons and herbs add a tangy freshness that goes beautifully with skate.

----

serves 4

4 small or 2 medium skate wings
cut in half (about 200g per
serving), skinned
2 tbsp olive oil
Small knob of butter
Sea salt and freshly ground black
pepper

For the sauce gribiche
4 hard-boiled eggs
200ml olive oil
3 tbsp good-quality wine vinegar
2 tbsp salted capers, rinsed and
roughly chopped
2 tbsp cornichons, finely chopped
2 tbsp finely chopped flat-leaf
parsley
1 tbsp finely chopped chervil
Few tarragon leaves, finely
chopped
Sea salt and freshly ground black
pepper

First make the sauce. Remove the yolks from the eggs and pound to a smooth paste. Finely chop the white and reserve for later.

Put the yolks in a bowl and slowly add the oil, stirring continuously to form an emulsion. As it starts to thicken, add the vinegar to loosen it, then continue to add the rest of the oil. When all the oil has been added, stir in the capers, cornichons, chopped herbs, chopped egg white and season with salt and pepper.

Preheat the oven to 220°C/425°F/gas mark 7.

Season the skate wings well on both sides.

Heat the oil and butter in an ovenproof frying pan large enough to fit the skate wings lying flat. When the oil is sizzling, lay the fish in the pan and fry for about 5 minutes on one side, shaking the pan gently every so often so the fish doesn't stick.

Put the pan into the oven and bake for 10-15 minutes (depending on the thickness of the fish) To test if the fish is cooked, pierce the thickest part with a skewer, which should slide easily through the flesh, otherwise cook for a little longer.

Serve with a generous dollop of the sauce, lemon to squeeze, buttered spring greens and boiled new potatoes.

Salmon with egg and lemon sauce

The sharpness of this lemon sauce works well with a rich, oily fish like salmon and brings out the freshness in the green vegetables. I like to use large spinach leaves, which has a stronger texture than the baby leaf variety. Otherwise broad beans, peas, chard or artichokes could be used.

————————————————————

serves 4

4 salmon fillets, about 200g each
2 tbsp olive oil
600g spinach, washed and thick
    stalks removed
4 egg yolks
Juice of 1 lemon
2 tbsp freshly chopped flat-leaf
    parsley
1 tbsp melted butter
Sea salt and freshly ground black
    pepper

Season the salmon fillets with salt and pepper and rub with a few drops of olive oil.

Heat the remaining oil in a frying pan over a medium-high heat until very hot, then fry the salmon for about 4–6 minutes on each side. When it is almost cooked through, transfer to a plate and keep warm.

Cook the spinach in plenty of boiling salted water for about a minute and then drain, reserving about 2–3 tablespoons of the cooking water.

Put the egg yolks, 1 tablespoon of the reserved spinach water and lemon juice in a small pan and place over a low heat. Heat gently, whisking all the time, until the sauce is almost boiling and has thickened slightly. Loosen the sauce if necessary with more spinach water. Remove from the heat and stir in the parsley and a little salt and pepper.

Toss the cooked spinach in the melted butter and season with salt and pepper.

Serve the salmon fillets with a pile of spinach and the sauce poured over the top.

Toad in the hole

serves 6

125g plain flour
150ml cold milk
150ml cold carbonated water
3 eggs, beaten
1½ tsp sea salt
6 tbsp oil (a mixture of sunflower
    and olive oil works well)
12 chipolatas (chipolatas give a
    better ratio of batter to sausage)

The batter for this classic supper dish is essentially the same as a Yorkshire pudding mix. The key to perfect toad in the hole is to have a sufficiently hot oven and to get the tray and oil really hot before putting the batter in.

The quantity of batter given here will also make 12 individual Yorkshire puddings: simply pour a little oil into the holes of a preheated muffin tray and pour the batter in. You will need to reduce the cooking time by about 15 minutes.

————————————————————

First make the batter. Sift the flour into a bowl and put the milk, water, beaten eggs and salt into a jug.

Make a well in the centre of the flour and pour the milk and egg mixture into it, a little at a time, stirring as you go to bring in the flour bit by bit. Keep pouring and continue to stir until you have a smooth batter.

Set aside to rest in the fridge for at least 30 minutes or over-night if necessary.

Preheat the oven to 200°C/400°F/gas mark 6.

Fry the chipolatas in 2 tablespoons of the oil until they are well browned all over.

Pour the remaining oil into a medium-sized roasting tin or baking tray and put into the oven to heat for a few minutes.

Carefully remove the tray filled with the hot oil and lay the sausages into it, scraping the delicious, gooey sediment produced by the sausages from the frying pan into the tray. Pour the batter all over them, so they become partially submerged and put it into the oven.

Bake for 20 minutes, then reduce the heat to 180°C/350°F/gas mark 4 and bake for a further 20 minutes, by which time the top will be golden and crisp and the batter will have risen dramatically. Resist the temptation to take the pudding out of the oven earlier when the top looks cooked, as the batter at the base won't be cooked enough.

PUDDINGS

Rhubarb and apricot soufflés

makes 8 soufflés, using individual
   200ml ramekins or soufflé dishes

20g unsalted butter
60g caster sugar, plus extra to dust
1½ tbsp cornflour
4 tbsp good-quality apricot jam
3 egg whites

For the rhubarb purée
400g rhubarb, washed and cut into
   short lengths
100g demerara sugar
Juice of 1 orange, plus a few strips
   of orange zest

If you don't want to be fussing around in the kitchen when you have guests, the soufflés can be made up to an hour in advance and kept in the fridge until ready to cook. Once cooked, these are fragile things so it's best to eat them as soon as they come out of the oven.

You will end up with more rhubarb purée than you need for the soufflés, but any leftover is delicious served with yoghurt and granola for breakfast.

First make the rhubarb purée. Preheat the oven to 150°C/300°F/gas mark 2.

Put all the ingredients in an ovenproof dish that fits the rhubarb in one layer and bake for about 20 minutes, or until the rhubarb is just tender. Remove and discard the strips of zest before blending to make a smooth purée. Set aside 250ml of purée and keep the rest in the fridge for another time.

Increase the oven temperature to 220°C/425°F/gas mark 7.

Heat the butter gently so it becomes very soft and then brush the inside and inside rim of the dishes with a generous layer of butter. This will help the soufflés to rise evenly. Dust the buttered dishes liberally with caster sugar and pour away any excess.

Mix the cornflour together with a teaspoon of the rhubarb purée and stir until dissolved. Put in a pan with the rest of the purée and bring to the boil, stirring until it thickens; this should only take a couple of minutes. Stir the jam into the rhubarb mixture and set aside to cool.

Whisk the egg whites until they begin to foam, then add the caster sugar and keep whisking until they become thick and smooth and form stiff peaks. Stir a tablespoon of the whites into the fruit mixture to loosen it and then gently fold in the rest.

Pour the mixture into the prepared dishes to about three-quarters full, gently smoothing over the top to create an even surface. Bake in the preheated oven for 8 minutes, or until the tops have risen dramatically and browned slightly. Serve immediately.

Also try
Use puréed raspberries, peaches or other fruits if rhubarb isn't available.

Baked sweet fluffy omelette with jam

serves 1-2

2 eggs, separated
2 tbsp jam (my favourites are apricot, damson or peach)
Pinch sea salt
10g unsalted butter

This is basically a 'souffléed' omelette, and for anyone who is scared of soufflés, it's a good introduction to the incredible fluffing effect of whisked egg whites. You can't go wrong because it is not supposed to rise much, it's just an omelette with some air in it.

————————————————

Preheat the oven to 200°C/400°F/gas mark 6.

Put the yolks in a small bowl and mix with the jam.

Put the whites in a large bowl and whisk just until they start to foam and increase in volume. They should be loose and bubbly, not quite at soft peak stage.

Add the yolk and jam mixture along with the salt to the whites and whisk together.

Melt the butter in an ovenproof frying pan over a medium heat until it bubbles.

Pour the omelette mix into the pan, tilting so it covers all of the base. Cook on a medium-high heat for about 30 seconds before sliding into the preheated oven.

After about 2-3 minutes, remove from the oven. Slide a spatula or palette knife under one side and gently fold over in half to reveal a browned and slightly caramelised bottom.

Pear and Marsala trifle

serves 6–8

Double quantity of crème
    patissière recipe (see page 31)
150ml Marsala
300ml double cream
60g blanched almonds, roughly
    chopped

For the sponge
3 eggs
90g caster sugar
75g plain flour, sifted
2 tbsp oil (sunflower, groundnut,
    grapeseed)
1 tsp vanilla extract
Pinch sea salt

For the poached pears
6 ripe Comice pears, peeled
    and cored
1 bay leaf
3 cloves
1 cinnamon stick
1 tsp vanilla extract
200ml Marsala

A well-built trifle is a beautiful thing to behold, especially if you can glimpse the layers through the sides of a glass bowl. Marsala is a fortified wine that comes from Sicily and is used in sweet desserts like zabaglione and tiramisu. As an alternative, you could use Madeira or sweet sherry. A trifle is one of the best puddings to make if you're entertaining; all the various stages can be made ahead and it can be assembled 24 hours before serving.

————————————————————

Preheat the oven to 180°C/350°F/gas mark 4 and line a 20×30cm sided baking tray with baking parchment.

First make the sponge. Beat the eggs and sugar together using an electric whisk until they reach ribbon stage. Add the sifted flour and fold to combine, then fold in the oil, vanilla extract and salt.

Pour the mixture into the prepared tin to form a thin layer and bake for about 15 minutes. A skewer inserted in the middle should come out clean. If not, return to the oven for another 5 minutes. Lay the cooked sheet of sponge on a wire rack to cool, peeling off the paper before it sticks.

Cut the pears into quarters and put them in a pan with the spices, vanilla extract and Marsala. Just cover with water and place over a medium-high heat. As soon as it comes to the boil, remove from the heat and allow to cool.

Make the crème patissière (see page 31).

Up to this point, everything can be made one or 2 days in advance.

When you are ready to assemble the trifle, roughly tear the sponge into pieces about the size of a large postage stamp, and lay them in the bottom of your chosen trifle bowl. Sprinkle the Marsala evenly over the sponge pieces.

Remove the pear pieces from their cooking liquor and lay them on the soaked sponge. (Any leftover cooking liquor can be used to poach dried fruit such as apricots and prunes.)

Spread the crème patissière over the pears.

Whip the cream to form soft peaks and spread over the top. You can now leave the trifle to sit for at least 24 hours in the fridge.

Serve sprinkle with the chopped almonds.

Bread and butter pudding

serves 4–6

5 slices of soft white bread, crusts
    on (use a medium size white
    bloomer or sandwich loaf)
About 40g unsalted butter,
    softened
25g chopped candied peel
25g sultanas
420ml full-fat milk
150ml double cream
80g caster sugar
1 vanilla pod, slit lengthways and
    seeds scraped out
Few gratings nutmeg
Zest of ½ orange
5 eggs, plus 3 egg yolks

The bread for this pudding should to be soft enough that the eggy custard completely soaks through it, making the layers of custard and bread almost indistinguishable from each other. *Pan de Mie*, white bloomer or leftover brioche (see page 48) all have good soaking qualities.

———————————————

Preheat the oven to 180°C/350°F/gas mark 4.

Cut the slices of bread in half diagonally and generously butter on both sides.

Find a baking dish which will fit the bread overlapping in two layers.

Lay half the bread in the bottom of dish, covering the surface but allowing for a little overlap. Sprinkle half of the candied peel and sultanas over the top. Repeat with the rest of the bread and sultanas and peel.

Pour the milk and cream into a large jug and add the sugar, vanilla seeds, nutmeg and orange zest. Whisk in all the eggs and pour the mixture all over the bread, making sure all the bread is soaked, especially near the crusts. If the bread reaches saturation point, save the rest of the liquid to pour over later.

Leave to soak for about 30 minutes and then add any remaining milk and egg mixture.

Cook in the preheated oven for about 25 minutes, or until slightly risen and crisp and brown on top.

Rhubarb meringue tartlets

makes 6 small tarts

300g rhubarb, washed and sliced
   into 5cm lengths
½ vanilla pod
15g brown sugar
Juice of 1 orange
1 quantity of sweet pastry (see
   page 28)

For the meringue
240g caster sugar
1 tbsp golden syrup
4 fresh eggs whites, at room
   temperature
Pinch fine sea salt
1 tsp cream of tartar

These individual tarts look so pretty with their peaks of soft meringue. The sharp taste of rhubarb and sweet topping creates the perfect contrast. You can make this as one large tart, but soft meringue can be tricky to cut into slices, so use a hot knife for a clean cut.

Both the rhubarb and pastry can be prepared in advance; the tart can also be served the day after baking if required.

————————————————

Preheat the oven to 150°C/300°F/gas mark 2.

Put the rhubarb pieces in a single layer in an oven dish. Scrape the seeds from the vanilla pod (put the pod into a jar of caster sugar to make vanilla sugar) and add the seeds to the rhubarb along with the sugar and orange juice. Bake for 30 minutes, or until just tender. Leave to cool.

Roll the pastry out on a floured surface to 5mm thick and use to line 6 loose-bottomed tartlet tins, approximately 12cm in diameter. Place in the fridge to rest for 20 minutes.

Line each tin with baking parchment and baking beans and bake blind for 15 minutes. Remove the paper and beans and return to the oven for another 15 minutes, or until the pastry is golden brown all over. Remove and leave to cool.

Pass the rhubarb through a sieve, reserving the liquid to make a sauce later. Mash the rhubarb pulp together to make a spreadable mixture and then spread over the base of each tart shell.

To make the meringue, put the sugar and golden syrup in a small pan and just cover with water. Heat gently, without stirring, until all the sugar has dissolved. Turn up the heat and boil, again without stirring, until syrup reaches 120°C (on a thermometer), this will take a couple of minutes.

Meanwhile whisk the egg whites in an electric mixer on low speed until it starts to foam, then add the salt and cream of tartar. Increase the speed to medium and whisk just until soft peaks start to form.

When the syrup is ready, start whisking the whites on low speed while pouring the hot syrup down the side of bowl in a slow, steady stream. Increase the speed to high and beat until mixture stops steaming or the bowl feels cool to the touch. This can take up to 10 minutes. During this time, the whites are cooking in the heat of the syrup and they will become very thick and smooth.

Spread the meringue over the tops of the tarts and make some little peaks on the top with your knife. Alternatively, use a piping bag and nozzle.

Bake in the oven for 10 minutes or use a blowtorch to lightly brown the tops.

Reduce the reserved rhubarb liquid in a small pan, adding a little more sugar if necessary, to serve alongside the finished tarts.

Also try
For a lemon meringue tart, follow the recipe as above, replacing the rhubarb with lemon curd (see page 114).

Crêpes Suzette

makes 12 crêpes, serving 6

For the crêpes
120g plain flour
Pinch fine sea salt
2 eggs
200ml milk
100ml water
20g melted unsalted butter,
    plus extra for frying

For the butter
100g unsalted butter, softened
2 tbsp caster sugar
1 orange
7 tbsp Grand Marnier, Cointreau,
    curaçao (or any orange-flavoured
    liqueur)

Crème fraîche, to serve (optional)

In old-fashioned restaurants, the waiter will prepare the crêpes at the table so the ostentatious flambéing can be seen to its greatest effect. Made at home, they can be as low key or as flamboyant as you choose. The real pleasure of this dessert is the sauce of the lightly caramelised sugar and butter, flavoured with orange juice and liqueur, which coats the crêpes. They are a classic and are well worth taking the trouble to make.

———————————————————

First make the crêpe batter. Sift the flour and salt into a bowl. (This will aerate the mixture and helps keep the batter light.) Make a well in the middle and add the eggs, milk and water. Use a whisk to stir the mixture from the centre, incorporating more flour as you go, until you have a smooth batter. Don't worry if you have a few lumps, they will dissolve. Leave to rest for at least 20 minutes. Stir in the melted butter just before you want to cook the crêpes.

Meanwhile, beat 80g of the butter in a bowl with the sugar until light and fluffy. Grate the zest of the orange into the bowl and mix well. Squeeze a tablespoon of the orange juice over the mixture and pour in a tablespoon of Grand Marnier and beat well. If it separates a bit, don't worry; it doesn't need to be completely unified. Leave at room temperature until needed.

To cook the crêpes: choose a non-stick or well-seasoned frying pan and get it really hot. Melt a small nugget of the remaining butter and pour in just enough batter to create a very thin layer all over the bottom of the pan. I like to use a ladle to do this, pouring while I tilt the pan sharply so it spreads all over.

Cook for about a minute or until the bottom is just starting to brown when you peep at it by lifting a corner with a palette knife. Turn it over to let it brown quickly on the other side before sliding onto a plate.

Repeat with the rest of the batter, stacking the cooked crêpes on top of each other as you go.

Allow the crêpes to cool before spreading a teaspoon of the butter mixture on each crêpe. Stack them again so the butter coats each side. (All of this can be done in advance.)

Just before you're ready to eat, heat the crêpe pan and lay the first crêpe into it. After a few seconds, fold it in half and in half again so it forms a triangle. Push it to the side of the pan and repeat with the next one. When there are 4 folded crêpes in the pan, allow them to cook for a few seconds to become a little crisp on the bottom, then remove to a warm plate and repeat with the others until all the crêpes are cooked in this way and arranged on the warming plate.

Then start to heat the remaining Grand Marnier in a separate small pan.

Add the rest of the butter to the crêpe pan and when it is bubbling, light the liqueur and pour it flaming into the melted butter. Swirl it around to make a sauce and pour this all over the crêpes.

I like to serve these with crème fraîche, which cuts through the richness of the sauce.

Isles flottantes

serves 4-6

For the meringues
2 egg whites
30g sugar
1 tsp vanilla extract

For the custard
200ml single cream
100ml full-fat milk, plus extra to
   top up
1 vanilla pod
3 whole eggs
2 egg yolks
80g caster sugar

For the caramel
225g sugar

These are fluffy, poached meringues floating in a pool of rich custard with a crisp caramel topping. They look impressive but aren't difficult to make. This tastes sublime and, like all the best puddings, can be made in advance.

Make the meringue by whisking the whites until they form soft peaks. Slowly add the sugar, continuing to whisk after each addition until it is all incorporated. Keep whisking until the mixture becomes thick and billowy with a silky texture. Add the vanilla extract and mix well.

Put the cream and the milk for the custard in a wide, shallow pan and bring to a simmer.

Using a dessertspoon, scoop large blobs of the meringue mixture and drop them into the hot cream, where they will bob around on the surface. Repeat with more spoonfuls until you have about 8-12, or however many will fit in the pan. Turn each of the meringue blobs over after about a minute and cook for another minute. Remove with a slotted spoon and transfer to a plate.

When all the meringues are cooked, strain the cream into a jug. Top it up with more milk to reach 300ml and pour this mixture into a pan. Slit the vanilla pod in half lengthways and scrape the seeds into the creamy milk. Bring this to the boil, then turn off the heat.

In a large bowl, whisk the eggs and yolks with the sugar until creamy. Slowly pour the hot milk into the bowl, whisking all the time, then return the whole lot to the pan and cook over a low heat, stirring all the time, until it starts to thicken - just enough to coat the back of a wooden spoon.

If the heat is too high and it starts to curdle, remove the custard from the heat immediately and whizz it with a handheld blender until smooth. If you don't have handheld blender, put the pan over iced water and whisk energetically by hand, then strain it to remove any lumps.

Pour the custard into a serving bowl and float the meringues on the surface.

Just before serving, make the caramel. Put the sugar in a pan and add just enough water to almost cover. Place over a high heat to bring it to the boil and cook until the sugar starts to colour and has a caramelised aroma.

Pour the caramel over the meringue islands - it will immediately set into a crackly covering.

Chocolate mousse corretto

This airy mousse is both light and rich at the same time, and the flavours of coffee, brandy and chocolate are perfect together. In Italy they call espresso with a shot of brandy *caffè corretto*, which means 'corrected' coffee.

_____

serves 4-6

100g good-quality dark chocolate, at least 70% cocoa solids, broken into small pieces
2 tbsp golden syrup
2 tsp espresso or very strong coffee
6 eggs, separated
1 tbsp brandy, Armagnac or cognac
Zest of ½ orange

Put about 5cm of water into a pan, over which a heatproof bowl will sit comfortably without touching the water, and bring to a simmer. Place the chocolate and golden syrup in the bowl and place over the water to gently melt the chocolate. Add the espresso.

Put the egg yolks in a bowl and add a tablespoon of water. When the chocolate has completely melted, pour it slowly into the egg yolk mixture, stirring continuously, and mix until smooth. Stir in the brandy and orange zest.

Put the egg whites in a clean, grease-free bowl or electric mixer with a whisk attachment and beat until they just form soft peaks. Take care not to over beat them or the mousse will become too stiff.

Stir in a spoonful of the whisked whites into the egg mixture to loosen it, then gently but thoroughly fold the rest in so they are completely combined.

Pour into small glasses, cups, ramekins or shallow serving dishes and put in the freezer for 20 minutes, then chill in the fridge for at least an hour, or until needed.

Chocolate, almond and pear Eton mess

serves 4-6

1 large, very ripe comice pear,
  peeled and cored
1 tsp lemon juice
40g dark chocolate, minimum
  70% cocoa solids
250ml double cream

For the meringue
4 medium egg whites (about 140g)
Pinch fine sea salt
280g caster sugar (or double the
  weight of the whites)
80g ground almonds

This is a richer version than the usual Eton Mess. The dark chocolate, almond meringue and pears make an even more delicious and decadent alternative.

For best results when whisking egg whites don't use the very freshest eggs. You can also store separated whites for a few days in the fridge, or freeze them and defrost when needed.

––––––––––––––––––––––––

Preheat the oven to 110°C/225°F/gas mark ¼.

Whisk the egg whites with the salt until they form soft peaks. Continue whisking, adding a few large spoonfuls of sugar at a time, making sure it's all incorporated before you add the next bit. The mixture should start to become silky and thick. When it's all incorporated, keep mixing for a few more minutes until glossy, thick and forming stiff peaks.

Fold the ground almonds into the mixture.

Lay a piece of baking parchment on a baking sheet and scoop large spoonfuls of the mixture onto the paper, leaving enough space around the sides so there is room for them to expand in the oven.

Bake for 1½-2 hours, or until dry and crisp and easy to lift off the paper. Allow to cool before crumbling into pieces.

Cut the pear into small pieces and sprinkle with the lemon juice to prevent discolouring. Slice the chocolate into thin shards, or grate it through the largest holes of the grater. Whisk the cream until it forms soft peaks, taking care not to over whisk.

Carefully fold the meringue pieces, pear and chocolate into the cream, reserving some chocolate. Serve in individual bowls or glasses with the reserved chocolate sprinkled on top.

This recipe can easily be made up to 2 hours in advance and kept in the fridge.

Profiteroles

serves 6

For the choux pastry
85g unsalted butter
220ml hot water (from the kettle)
105g plain flour, sifted
Pinch sea salt
4 eggs

To finish
160g dark chocolate, minimum
   70% cocoa solids
2 tbsp sugar
40g unsalted butter
50ml water
400ml double cream
2 tbsp icing sugar

A mountain of chocolate covered profiteroles, oozing with cream is a beautiful sight. They suit being made in advance, making them the perfect party pudding. Surprisingly, choux is also one of the easiest pastries to make; just make sure you use a heavy pan with deep sides so there's plenty of room to beat the mixture.

_____

Preheat the oven to 200°C/400°F/gas mark 6 and have a bowl of iced water ready.

Put the butter and hot water for the pastry into a pan and slowly bring to the boil. The butter should all be melted by the time the water boils.

As soon as the water is at a rolling boil, remove from the heat and tip in the sifted flour. Add the salt, and working quickly, beat the mixture firmly with a wooden spoon. Don't be scared if it's lumpy at first, it will soon become smooth and come away from the sides to form a soft blob.

Transfer to a clean bowl and cool to room temperature. To speed this up, sit the bowl over the bowl of iced water and stir occasionally.

Once cool, use a wooden spoon to beat the eggs in one at a time. After the initial lumps, the mixture will again become smooth, silky and soft. A dollop of it should drop reluctantly off a spoon.

Line a baking sheet with baking parchment. Spoon the choux mixture into a piping bag fitted with a large nozzle and pipe balls of mixture, about the size of a walnut, onto the paper. Make sure they are well spaced apart as they will expand during cooking.

Bake in the preheated oven for 20 minutes or until the tops are golden brown and have become crisp. Transfer to a wire rack to cool.

Put the chocolate, sugar, butter and water in a pan and melt very gently over a low heat until it has a smooth pouring consistency. If it looks too thick, add a little more water.

Meanwhile, whip the cream with the icing sugar until it just forms soft peaks. Be careful not to over whip it. Put the cream into a piping bag fitted with a small nozzle and pipe cream into each profiterole.

Stack each filled profiterole onto a serving dish and when the chocolate is melted, use a dessertspoon to pour a little over the top of each profiterole, so it covers the top and dribbles down the sides. Allow to cool and for the chocolate to set before serving.

Also try
You can serve these little profiteroles halved and filled with balls of zabaglione ice cream (see page 181) and the remaining hot chocolate sauce in a jug to pass around at the table.

Custard tart

makes 1 tart, serving 6-8

1 quantity of sweet pastry (see
    page 28)
7 egg yolks
50g caster sugar
450ml double cream
1 vanilla pod
Nutmeg, for grating

A custard tart is one of the finest puddings - crisp pastry filled
with a rich, wobbly custard and topped with grated nutmeg.
I usually like it best in its simplest form, but when raspberries,
rhubarb or sweet, juicy cherries are in season, they make an
excellent addition, creating little pockets of fruitiness and an
even prettier pudding; just leave out the nutmeg.

Prepare the pastry and use it to line a 23cm loose-bottomed
tart tin. Chill in the fridge for 20 minutes while you preheat
the oven to 150°C/300°F/gas mark 2.

Line the pastry case with baking parchment and fill with
baking beans. Bake blind for 15 minutes. Remove the paper
and beans and return to the oven for a further 15 minutes,
until golden and sandy textured. Leave to cool while you
prepare the custard.

In a large bowl, whisk the yolks and sugar until the sugar has
dissolved.

Put the cream into a pan, slit the vanilla pod lengthways and
scrape the seeds into the cream. (Place the empty pod in a jar
of caster sugar to make vanilla sugar.)

Heat the cream until it just starts to come to the boil then pour
it in a thin stream into the yolks, whisking as you do. Return
the whole mixture to the pan and heat very gently, stirring
continuously, until it thickens slightly.

Strain the custard into a jug. If there are any lumps in the
custard (caused by cooking it at too high a temperature), give
it a whizz with a handheld blender until it is completely
smooth.

Pour the custard into the baked tart shell and return to the
oven for 35-40mins or until the filling feels firm but still a
little wobbly to the touch. Grate the nutmeg all over the
surface and allow to cool completely. (The custard will set
further.) Once cooked, cut and serve.

Also try
Scatter 100g of any of the following fruit evenly into the
baked tart shell before pouring the custard over and baking:
- Ripe raspberries
- Stoned cherries, macerated in brandy
- Cooked rhubarb pieces, strained to remove excess liquid
- Prunes soaked in 200ml strong Earl Grey tea, drained and
  then heated gently with 2 tbsp brandy.

Blackberry ice cream

serves 8-10

600ml double cream
400ml milk
1 vanilla pod
6 egg yolks
200g caster sugar
500g blackberries (or other
    soft fruit)

Homemade ice cream is one of the greatest pleasures. I first made this after a very successful day's blackberry picking and have never looked back. This recipe can also be used as a template for any soft fruit ice cream like raspberries, loganberries or blackcurrants, just adjust the sugar content as necessary.

If you really love ice cream, it's a good idea to invest in an ice cream maker; they can be purchased relatively inexpensively and will make your homemade ice cream even better.

_____

Put the cream and milk in a pan. Slit the vanilla pod in half lengthways and scrape the seeds into the pan, adding the pod as well. Bring to the boil then immediately take off the heat.

In a large bowl, beat together the egg yolks and sugar until pale and thick. It's best to do this in an electric mixer; this will make a lighter, creamier ice cream.

Remove the vanilla pod from the hot milk and cream mixture. Pour the mixture over the yolks in a thin dribble, mixing all the time so that the yolks combine without curdling. Then return the mixture to the heat, stirring until it starts to thicken.

Remove from the heat and allow to cool to room temperature.

In a blender or food processor, blitz the blackberries to a pulp and pass through a sieve to get a smooth purée. Stir this into the custard mixture and taste. Add a little more sugar if necessary - when it is frozen it won't taste quite as sweet.

Churn in an ice cream machine until just frozen then put in the freezer for at least an hour before serving.

If you are churning the ice cream by hand, allow it to chill for about an hour in the freezer, then remove it and beat or whisk it vigorously to break up the ice crystals. Repeat this every hour or so until it is nearly solid. Return to the freezer until needed, although this is best eaten within 2 days, while the flavours are at their freshest.

Roasted almond ice cream

This is easily my favourite ice cream and it tastes just as good in mid-summer as it does after a lunch in winter. (Pictured on page 177.)

——————————————————————

serves 8-10

200g blanched almonds
2 tbsp icing sugar
Large pinch sea salt
600ml double cream
400ml milk
1 vanilla pod
6 egg yolks
180g caster sugar

Preheat the oven to 150°C/300°F/gas mark 2.

Put the almonds, icing sugar and salt into a baking tray and toss well until the almonds are all coated.

Roast in the oven for 10-15 minutes, or until the almonds are just starting to toast and become nutty brown. Transfer to a plate to cool, then chop roughly.

Put the cream and milk in a pan. Slit the vanilla pod in half lengthways and scrape the seeds into the pan then add the pod as well. Bring to the boil then immediately take off the heat.

In a large bowl, beat together the egg yolks and sugar until pale and thick. It's best to do this in an electric mixer; this will make a lighter, creamier ice cream.

Remove the vanilla pod from the hot milk and cream mixture. Pour the mixture over the yolks in a thin dribble, mixing all the time so that the yolks combine without curdling. Then return the mixture to the heat, stirring until it starts to thicken. Strain through a sieve and cool.

When the custard is cool, churn in an ice cream machine until just frozen then add the chopped almonds and continue to churn until almost solid. Put in the freezer for at least an hour before serving.

If you are churning the ice cream by hand, allow it to chill for about an hour in the freezer, then remove it and beat or whisk it vigorously to break up the ice crystals. Repeat this every hour or so until it is nearly solid. Then fold in the nuts and leave to freeze completely.

Fresh ice cream is best eaten within a couple of days while the texture and flavour are at their best.

Zabaglione ice cream

serves 4-6

6 egg yolks
90g sugar
25ml Marsala
2 egg whites
100ml double cream

The Italians gave us zabaglione - a sweet, foamy custard flavoured with Marsala wine. It's not difficult to make, but it does require some whisking over a hot pan (not something you want to do while your guests are sitting at the table). So I like to make it as an ice cream, which can be chilled until needed. A couple of scoops make an elegant pudding or serve it alongside a rich chocolate cake or warm poached fruit as a decadent alternative to cream.

Unlike most custard-based ice creams, you don't need to churn this one; the egg whites keep it fluffy and light while it freezes. Made in the morning, it will be perfectly frozen in time for supper and, like all homemade ice cream, it's best eaten within a few days while the consistency is still creamy and soft.

Choose a heatproof bowl that will fit comfortably over a pan of water without the base of the bowl touching the water.

Have a large bowl of iced water at the ready.

Put about 3cm of water into the pan and bring to the boil. Put the yolks and sugar in the heatproof bowl and set it over the pan of boiling water. Using a large whisk, beat until pale and creamy, then add the Marsala. Continue to whisk for about 10 minutes, or until the mixture has thickened and reached ribbon consistency (when lifted the whisk leaves a 'ribbon' trail over the surface).

Put the bowl over the iced water and continue whisking until it cools.

In a separate, very clean bowl, whisk the eggs to soft peaks. Clean the bowl and then whisk the cream until soft peaks form but don't over whisk or the ice cream will be too heavy.

Fold the cream into the yolks and add a spoonful of whisked whites to loosen the mixture slightly before gently folding in the rest.

Pour the mixture into a metal cake tin or tray, bearing in mind that the deeper the level, the longer it will take to freeze.

Wrap tightly in cling film and freeze for at least 4 hours, or until set.

Baked apple pudding

serves 4

220g unsalted butter
2 lemons
4 medium Bramley or cooking
    apples, peeled, cored and cut
    into quarters
1 bay leaf
2 cloves
180g caster sugar
2 eggs, separated
2 tbsp plain flour
Pinch ground cinnamon
200g fine white breadcrumbs

This is an old-fashioned pudding of puréed, spiced apple with a fluffy, crunchy top. The recipe uses breadcrumbs, instead of flour, to create the cake mixture. It's a good excuse to seek out a better quality loaf of white sourdough, or pain de campagne and turn the leftovers into crumbs.

————————————————————

Preheat the oven to 180°C/350°F/gas mark 4 and butter a deep 20cm ovenproof dish.

Melt 20g of the butter in a pan over a low heat. Pare the zest of one of the lemons into large strips and add to the pan, along with the squeezed juice. Add the apples, bay leaf and cloves. Cover and cook for 10-15 minutes or until the apples are completely soft and collapsing.

Push the cooked apple through a large sieve or colander, discarding the bay leaf, cloves and zest, to make a smooth purée. Set aside to cool.

Beat the remaining butter and sugar until light and fluffy, add the egg yolks and mix well. Fold in the flour, cinnamon, breadcrumbs, and grate in the zest of the remaining lemon.

Whisk the egg whites until they form stiff peaks. Stir a large spoonful of them into the cake mixture to loosen it, then carefully fold in the remaining whites.

Put the apple purée into the bottom of the prepared dish and spread the cake mixture on top. Bake for 45 minutes or until golden and slightly risen.

Serve hot, straight from the dish, with cream on the side.

Steamed marmalade pudding

makes 1 pudding, serving 4-6

140g unsalted butter, softened, plus extra for greasing
200g plain flour, plus extra for dusting
125g caster sugar
Zest of ½ orange
3 eggs
1½ tsp baking powder
150ml milk
170g marmalade or jam (about 5 tbsp)

This classic steamed sponge pudding is given a topping of gooey jam. I love using marmalade for its bitter-sweet flavour, but it's a great way to use whatever your favourite jam is. Try raspberry, damson or apricot if you don't like marmalade.

Preheat the oven to 160°C/320°F/gas mark 2 and butter a 1.2-litre pudding basin. Dust the inside with about a tablespoon of flour and tip out the excess.

Cream together the butter, sugar and orange zest in an electric stand mixer until smooth and pale.

Add the eggs, one at a time, beating well between each one. Sift in the flour and baking powder and fold everything together using a spatula or metal spoon. Gradually stir in the milk to make the mixture loose enough that it drops easily from the spoon.

Put the marmalade or jam into the prepared pudding basin, followed by the sponge mixture.

Place a sheet of greaseproof paper on top of a sheet of foil and make a pleat by folding a crease in both the foil and paper. Turn over so the foil is uppermost and place over the top of the basin. Press it firmly around the rim of the bowl and secure with a long piece of string. Place in a roasting tray and pour boiling water into the tray to come about 6cm up the sides. Steam in the preheated oven for 2 hours.

Carefully remove the foil and paper and check the sponge is cooked – a skewer inserted into the middle should come out clean. If not, re-cover and return to the oven.

Put a plate over the top of the pudding basin and invert to turn out.

Serve with crème fraîche, cream or custard.

SAUCES

Mayonnaise

Mayonnaise is a magical emulsion of egg yolk and oil and is the beginning of many wonderful sauces, including garlicky aioli or mustardy remoulade. Homemade mayonnaise is really simple to make and the flavour is incomparably better than anything shop bought.

Whether served on an elegant shellfish plate, as a dip for crudités or a creamy layer in a sandwich, mayonnaise is as useful as it is delicious. Fresh homemade mayonnaise will keep for up to 3 days in the fridge.

Tips for perfect mayonnaise
· Use cold eggs to help stabilise the emulsion.
· If your mayonnaise splits, try adding a teaspoon of cold water and giving it a good whisk. Failing that, start with a new yolk, and pour the split sauce into it drip by drip, whisking continuously.

Classic mayonnaise

makes enough for 4 servings

2 egg yolks
1 tsp Dijon mustard
290ml olive oil, or a mild oil such
    as sunflower or groundnut
1-2 tsp good-quality wine vinegar
Sea salt and freshly ground black
    pepper

Put the yolks in a bowl with the mustard and whisk together. Add a few drops of oil and continue to whisk the yolks, while adding a little more oil, drop by drop, until an emulsion starts to form. Then pour the oil in a thin stream, whisking constantly until the mixture thickens. Use the vinegar to loosen the emulsion if it gets too thick. When all the oil is added, taste the mayonnaise and add more vinegar if necessary. Season with salt and pepper.

Italian-style mayonnaise

makes enough for 4 servings

2 egg yolks
290ml Italian olive oil
1-2 tsp lemon juice or water
Sea salt and freshly ground black
    pepper

Put the yolks in a bowl and whisk the oil, drop by drop, until an emulsion starts to form. Then pour the oil in a thin stream, whisking constantly until the mixture thickens. Use the lemon juice or water to loosen the emulsion if it gets too thick. When all the oil is added, taste the mayonnaise and add more lemon juice if necessary. Season with salt and pepper.

Garlic mayonnaise

makes enough for 4 servings

2 egg yolks
4 cloves garlic, crushed to a paste
    with salt
290ml olive oil
1-2 tsp lemon juice or water
Sea salt and freshly ground black
    pepper

Put the yolks in a bowl with the crushed garlic and whisk in the oil, drop by drop, until an emulsion starts to form. Then pour the oil in a thin stream, whisking constantly until the mixture thickens. Use the lemon juice or water to loosen the emulsion if it gets too thick. When all the oil is added, taste the mayonnaise and add more lemon juice if necessary. Season with salt and pepper.

Hollandaise sauce

makes enough for 4 servings

4 egg yolks
220g cold unsalted butter, cut into
    small cubes
1–2 tbsp lemon juice, to taste
Sea salt and white pepper

Unlike mayonnaise, the egg yolks are cooked to a creamy consistency with butter and the sauce is served either warm or at room temperature, never cold. It can be made in advance and stored in the fridge, but it should be heated before serving.

_____

Place a small heatproof bowl over a pan of gently simmering water, making sure the base of the bowl does not touch the water. Put the yolks, salt and a cube of the butter into the bowl and heat, stirring with a wooden spoon, until the butter is melted and the yolks are just starting to get hot. Then beat in the rest of the butter, one cube at a time, stirring continuously.

When the mixture has thickened and become light and creamy, remove it from the heat and beat in the lemon juice, a tablespoon at a time, to taste. Season with salt and pepper.

Béarnaise sauce

makes enough for 4 servings

3 tbsp good-quality white wine
    vinegar
½ tsp black peppercorns
1 bay leaf
1 blade of mace (optional)
1 shallot, finely chopped
4 egg yolks
220g cold unsalted butter, cut
    into small cubes
1 tbsp chopped chervil
1 tbsp chopped tarragon
Sea salt and white pepper

Béarnaise is another classic sauce, similar to hollandaise, but with the subtle flavour of shallots.

_____

Put the vinegar, peppercorns, bay leaf, mace (if using) and chopped shallot in a small pan. Bring to the boil and reduce until there is only about 1 tablespoon of vinegar in the pan. Take off the heat and discard the solids, leaving just the liquid.

Place a small heatproof bowl over a pan of gently simmering water, making sure the base of the bowl does not touch the water. Put the yolks, the shallot vinegar, salt and a cube of the butter into the bowl and heat, stirring with a wooden spoon, until the butter is melted and the yolks are just starting to get hot. Then, one cube at a time, beat in the rest of the butter, until it is all melted and well mixed. When the mixture has thickened and become light and creamy, remove it from the heat and stir in the chopped chervil and tarragon then season with salt and pepper.

Fonduta sauce

makes enough for 4 servings

170g fontina cheese, grated
300ml milk
15g unsalted butter
1 egg
3 egg yolks
Pinch white pepper

Fonduta sauce is a decadent, rich, hot cheese custard, made using fontina cheese, produced in the Val D'Aosta and Piedmont regions in Northern Italy. One of the finest ways to enjoy rare white truffle is to eat it shaved over hot fonduta sauce. However, you can use fonduta in many other ways that don't require such extravagant ingredients: try pouring over grilled polenta with some roasted radicchio. I like to use up any cold leftover fonduta up by shaping it into balls, covering with breadcrumbs and frying to make melting cheese bites. A much lighter version of fonduta, using Parmesan and crème fraîche, is given as a pasta sauce on page 132.

_____

Put the grated cheese in a bowl and add the milk; leave to soak for at least 1-2 hours.

Melt the butter in a pan over a medium heat and add the milk and cheese, whisking until the cheese is completely melted.

Remove from the heat and add the egg and egg yolks, whisking all the time. Add the pepper and keep whisking until you have a smooth sauce.

Dragoncella

makes enough for 4 servings

1 thin slice of stale sourdough
    bread, crusts removed
4 hard-boiled eggs
20g tarragon, finely chopped
4 anchovy fillets, finely chopped
1 tbsp salted capers, rinsed, drained
    and finely chopped
3 tbsp good-quality white wine
    vinegar
6-8 tbsp olive oil

Hard-boiled eggs are a valuable ingredient used to enrich sauces, such as the herby, chopped egg and sauce gribiche on pages 122 and 142 (also pictured here). Dragoncella (which means tarragon in Italian) is another example of this, where cooked egg yolk is combined with the powerful anise flavour of tarragon. This sauce is excellent served with poached chicken or other boiled meats such as salted beef.

Try to use a firm textured bread, like sourdough, that holds its structure and doesn't dissolve into the sauce.

Preheat the oven to 180°C/350°F/gas mark 4.

Tear the bread into very small pieces, place in a oven dish and bake for 10-15 minutes until completely dried out and crumbly.

Remove the egg yolks (you do not need the whites for this recipe) and chop into small pieces.

Place the eggs in a bowl with the tarragon, chopped anchovies, capers, bread and vinegar. Mix together well and then stir in the olive oil to make a sauce.

DRINKS

Whisky sour

serves 2

50ml Scotch whisky
50ml lemon juice
1-2 tbsp sugar syrup (I like Monin
    Gomme syrup)
Dash Angostura bitters
1 egg white
2 maraschino cherries
Ice cubes

Traditionally whisky sour is made with Bourbon, but I much prefer it made with Scotch, which is less sweet. You don't have to use either the maraschino cherries or the Angostura bitters, but they give the drink a beautiful pink hue.

–––––––––––––––––––––––––

Chill a couple of tumblers or your favourite cocktail glasses by filling them with ice and water.

Put all the ingredients except the cherries and ice into a cocktail shaker and shake vigorously. The egg white will become light and foamy.

Then add a handful of ice cubes and shake a few more times.

Empty the ice and water from the glasses and put a cherry in the bottom of each glass before straining the chilled cocktail over the top.

Bees knees

serves 2

50ml gin
50ml lemon juice
2-3 tbsp good-quality runny honey
1 egg white
Ice cubes

Something magical happens when the flowery flavours of honey and the botanicals of gin combine. Measurements for cocktails should just be a rough guideline; there are so many variables, including which gin or honey you use. It's all about how strong and sweet you like your drink so have a few attempts until you get it just how you like it.

———————————————————

Chill a couple of tumblers or your favourite cocktail glasses by filling them with ice and water.

Put all the ingredients (without any ice) in a cocktail shaker and shake vigorously. The egg white will become light and foamy.

Then add a handful of ice cubes and shake a few more times.

Empty the ice and water from the glasses and strain the chilled cocktail into them.

Prairie oyster

serves 1

1 tsp Worcestershire sauce
Few dashes Tabasco
1 tbsp tomato juice
Sea salt and freshly ground black
   pepper
1 egg

I like to add a little tomato juice to mine, but the purists may disagree.

———————————————————

Mix all the ingredients, except the egg, together until well combined. Pour into a glass and slide the egg into it.

Down in one.

Egg nog

serves 4

3 eggs, separated
30g sugar
2 tbsp your chosen alcohol
   (Bourbon works very well,
   or brandy or rum)
100ml double cream
Ice cubes
Nutmeg, for grating

Despite the richness of the ingredients, this actually tastes deliciously lighter than you might expect. Just make sure you serve it chilled.

_____

Whisk the yolks and sugar in a bowl until they are thick and creamy and increased in volume. Continue to whisk while you add the alcohol.

Chill in the fridge for at least 30 minutes to allow the flavours to develop.

When you are ready to serve it, whisk the cream until it forms soft peaks and fold it into the chilled yolk mixture.

In a separate, very clean bowl, whisk the egg whites to stiff peaks and then stir a spoonful of them into the cream and yolk mixture before folding in the remainder.

Fill 4 glasses with lots of ice and pour the mixture over. Grate over the nutmeg and serve immediately.

Index

Page numbers in *italic* refer to the illustrations

Acknowledgements

I'd like to thank Amanda Harris at Orion Publishing for commissioning this book and answering the eternal question - which came first? Her encouragement, confidence and support is invaluable. Thanks to Kate Wanwimolruk, my editor, for her enthusiasm and unfailing attention to detail and schedules, to Clare Skeats for her beautiful and clever design, Sara Griffin and Lucie Stericker for masterminding the photo shoot.

The magical touch of photographer Paul Winch-Furness has given all the colour and vibrancy to the recipes that I could wish for, and with the talented hand of Claire Ptak styling the shots, the book has come alive.

Thanks also to Jake, Jay and Sanaz for their help on the shoots, to all of my tasters and testers, especially Lesley. Thank you to Hugo, for being my greatest encouragement, critic and support. And finally to all those hens, for their endless hard work.

First published in Great Britain in 2015
by Weidenfeld & Nicolson, an imprint of the
Orion Publishing Group Ltd
Orion House, 5 Upper St Martin's Lane
London WC2H 9EA
An Hachette UK Company

10 9 8 7 6 5 4 3 2 1

A CIP catalogue record for this book is available from the
British Library.

ISBN: 978-0-297-87160-6

Design © Clare Skeats
Photography © Paul Winch-Furness
Styling by Claire Ptak
Copy-edited by Clare Sayer
Project edited by Kate Wanwimolruk
Index by Hilary Bird

Printed and bound in China

The Orion Publishing Group's policy is to use papers that are natural,
renewable and recyclable products and made from wood grown in
sustainable forests. The logging and manufacturing processes are
expected to conform to the environmental regulations of the
country of origin.

www.orionbooks.co.uk